Democracy
Without Borders?

To Andrea & Michael,
With love and
appreciation,
Marc

Democracy Without Borders?

Global Challenges to Liberal Democracy

Marc F. Plattner

ROWMAN & LITTLEFIELD PUBLISHERS, INC.
Lanham • *Boulder* • *New York* • *Toronto* • *Plymouth, UK*

ROWMAN & LITTLEFIELD PUBLISHERS, INC.

Published in the United States of America
by Rowman & Littlefield Publishers, Inc.
A wholly owned subsidary of The Rowman & Littlefield Publishing Group, Inc.
4501 Forbes Boulevard, Suite 200, Lanham, Maryland 20706
www.rowmanlittlefield.com

Estover Road
Plymouth PL6 7PY
United Kingdom

British Library Cataloguing in Publication Information Available

Library of Congress Cataloging-in-Publication Data

Plattner, Marc F., 1945–
    Democracy without borders? : global challenges to liberal democracy / Marc F.
Plattner.
      p. cm.
    Includes bibliographical references.
    ISBN-13: 978-0-7425-5925-7 (cloth : alk. paper)
    ISBN-10: 0-7425-5925-4 (cloth : alk. paper)
    ISBN-13: 978-0-7425-5926-4 (pbk. : alk. paper)
    ISBN-10: 0-7425-5926-2 (pbk. : alk. paper)
    1. Democracy. 2. Globalization. 3. Liberalism. I. Title.
JC423.P533 2008
321.8—dc22   2007024126

Printed in the United States of America

∞™ The paper used in this publication meets the minimum requirements of
American National Standard for Information Sciences—Permanence of Paper
for Printed Library Materials, ANSI/NISO Z39.48-1992.

To Jacqui, David, and Laura

Contents

Acknowledgments

This compact volume is the fruit of a long period of thinking, labor, and experience. As a consequence, the list of people and institutions that I wish to thank is extensive; even so, I will no doubt fail to include many who deserve to be noted here.

Since 1984 my professional life has revolved around the National Endowment for Democracy (NED), an institution that I joined shortly after its launching. Though I speak a bit about NED in the opening chapter of this book, I try to do so there with an appropriate degree of detachment. But here I feel free to say that it is truly a remarkable organization, one that owes much of its success and its distinctiveness to Carl Gershman, who has been its president since the beginning. Carl has created an institutional ethos that is at once passionately committed to supporting activists on the front lines in the struggle for democracy *and* extraordinarily open to intellectual debate—a rare combination that is not easy to maintain. It is this ethos—fully supported by NED's board of directors—that has enabled the *Journal of Democracy* to flourish under NED's aegis and within its offices.

Though I am deeply devoted to NED's overall mission, my real love is editing the *Journal of Democracy*. And like Carl, Larry Diamond, the cofounder and coeditor of the *Journal*, has been a true friend and a wonderful colleague for many years. Even after all this time, I am continually amazed by the breadth of Larry's knowledge, his indefatigable energy (despite his repeated claims of being "overwhelmed"), and his unbelievable productivity.

The *Journal* has greatly benefited as well from the contributions of a superb editorial board and a remarkably able staff. I particularly want to note the contribution of a founding member of the board, the late Seymour Martin Lipset, who helped to bring the *Journal* into being and to shape and inspire its intellectual orientation. Among the staff, I must single out exec-utive editor Phil Costopoulos, who has been with us since the beginning (except for a brief hiatus). Phil deserves much of the credit for the *Journal*'s literary merits, and his fine hand is visible in the chapters in this volume that originally appeared as articles in the *Journal*. Over the years, I have had a number of excellent assistants, but I owe special thanks to Eric Kramon, without whose help this volume would never have been completed. I am also grateful to my new assistant Marta Kalabinski and to Tom Warner for their assistance with the index.

There are several other organizations I wish to thank. The Smith Richard-son Foundation awarded a grant that enabled me to spend eight months in 2002–2003 as a visiting professor at the Robert Schuman Centre for Ad-vanced Studies at the European University Institute in Florence. This was an ideal setting in which to do the concentrated reading and research essential for completing this volume, and I am grateful to Helen Wallace, then direc-tor of the Schuman Centre, and to Jan Zielonka for making my stay there possible. Several of the essays included in this volume were initially pre-sented at the annual meetings of the Institute for Political Studies of the Portuguese Catholic University, and I profited greatly from the discussions that took place on those occasions. This annual meeting is a wonderful event that reflects the guiding spirit of the Institute's director, my good friend João Carlos Espada. Finally, I am grateful to Michael McFaul, the di-rector of Stanford's Center on Democracy, Development, and the Rule of Law, for hosting me as a visiting scholar as I put the final touches on this volume in the summer of 2007.

I owe a still deeper debt of gratitude to an extraordinary group of teach-ers with whom I had the privilege to study as a graduate student at Cornell. I learned a great deal from Walter Berns, Werner Dannhauser, and Myron Rush, but it was my thesis advisor Allan Bloom who principally shaped my education. He was an unparalleled teacher who attracted many of Cornell's best students, a number of whom remain among my closest friends.

This book is dedicated to my wife Jacqui Stark and my children, David and Laura Plattner. Jacqui happens to be a gifted editor who has given me some very useful editorial advice, but that is the least of what she has pro-vided. Thanks to the three of them, I can say that my family life has been a source of sustenance and joy.

I

INTRODUCTION

1

The Triumphs and Travails
of Democracy

The essays that follow constitute a series of attempts to understand the essential nature of modern liberal democracy. This book may be said to have three major elements. The first is simply an ongoing effort to assess the progress of liberal democracy around the world and to evaluate its future prospects. While this concern is indeed visible throughout the volume, it is the special focus of chapter 2 and of the concluding chapter. The two remaining elements of the book consist of reflections on a pair of key theoretical issues that emerged from policy debates about the advances and setbacks of democratization over the past quarter century: One is the relationship between liberalism and democracy (the two essential components of liberal democracy), which is addressed in chapters 3 through 5. The other is the relationship between liberal democracy and the nation-state, which is addressed in chapters 6 through 9. Very crudely stated, the contention of this book is that we cannot hope to enjoy liberalism (at least in today's world) unless it is accompanied by democracy, and we cannot enjoy liberal democracy outside the framework of the nation-state.

None of these essays fits neatly into conventional American genres either of academic or of popular writing. They do not aim at advancing an academic "literature," and they lack the heavy reliance on contemporary scholarship that characterizes most academic writing today. They perhaps come closest to what might be called "public policy essays," and yet for the most part they do not offer specific solutions to current problems. Moreover, they draw much more extensively on the classic works of political philosophy than do most policy essays or works in academic political science (except, of course, for scholarly studies in political philosophy). At the same time, however, these essays are thoroughly immersed in the events and the policy debates of the moment, which they typically take as their starting point.

I did not intentionally set out to write in this somewhat unusual manner, so I suppose that it is a product of my education and my subsequent experience in the world. Trained in political philosophy, I wrote a doctoral dissertation on Jean-Jacques Rousseau's *Discourse on the Origin and Foundations of Inequality Among Men* (the so-called *Second Discourse*). Yet even before finishing the dissertation, I decided that I did not want to devote my life's work to the exegesis of philosophic texts, or indeed to pursue an academic career at all. Instead, I wound up entering the world of public policy and international affairs—as an editor, a foundation program officer, and a government official at the United States Mission to the United Nations. In all these roles, and in my own writing, I was partly in the business of trying to present serious ideas in a way that was accessible and persuasive to a general audience. At the same time, I found myself constantly having recourse to the works of the great philosophic authors who had informed my education—not because it was fashionable to refer to them (it was more likely to be unfashionable), but because I found their analysis of fundamental questions to be more lucid and penetrating than anyone else's.

In September 1984 I moved to Washington to take up a position at the newly established National Endowment for Democracy (NED), and I have been working there in a variety of capacities ever since. From 1984 to 1989 I directed the Endowment's grants program, which provides assistance to groups working to establish and consolidate democracy in countries around the world. Then in 1989, together with Larry Diamond of Stanford's Hoover Institution, I founded and became coeditor of the *Journal of Democracy*, a quarterly publication devoted to the exploration of democracy's global prospects and the problems confronting it. And in 1994 Diamond and I launched the NED's International Forum for Democratic Studies, a larger research enterprise aimed at fostering interchange between scholars and practitioners of democracy and at producing a series of studies on democratization. Since that time the Forum has published some twenty books analyzing democracy in its various thematic aspects and regional manifestations. So for more than two decades I have had a remarkable perch from which to observe the triumphs and travails of democracy during the period of its greatest global expansion.

THE GLOBAL RESURGENCE OF DEMOCRACY

The twentieth century witnessed some of the most terrible wars and crimes in human history, but also remarkable progress in the global spread of democracy. When asked, near the century's end, what had been its most important development, Nobel prize-winning economist Amartya Sen con-cluded: "I would argue that in the distant future, when people look back at what happened in this century, they will find it difficult not to accord pri-macy to the emergence of democracy as the preeminently acceptable form of government."[1] Sen's remark applies both to the realm of practice and to that of ideas. As for the former, in 1900 there were no countries that "en-joyed competitive party politics with universal suffrage," and only 12.4 per-cent of humanity lived under a "somewhat democratic" government with suffrage limited to males. By 2000, universal suffrage was pervasive, and over 58 percent of humanity lived under "democratically elected leader-ship."[2] As for the realm of ideas, Sen noted that, while "democracy is not yet universally practiced, nor indeed universally accepted, in the general cli-mate of world opinion democratic governance has now achieved the status of being taken to be generally right."[3]

Yet democracy's global preeminence in both legitimacy and in practice certainly seemed far from evident at the century's three-quarter mark. In fact, the 1970s marked a low point for democracy in the post–World War II period. Most of the new democracies established by the departing colonial powers had unraveled, Soviet influence was growing, and the success of OPEC in the 1973 oil crisis was thought to be a harbinger of the economic decline of the advanced democracies. In 1975, Indira Gandhi declared a "state of emergency" in India, suddenly dropping the largest and most important non-Western democracy from the ranks of free countries. No less a defender of freedom than Daniel Patrick Moynihan was led to muse that liberal democracy as a form of government belonged to the past, and not the future.

Only in retrospect did it become clear that at that very moment a global resurgence of democracy was beginning in Southern Europe, with the transi-tions to democracy in Portugal, Spain, and Greece. What Samuel P. Hunting-ton has famously labeled the "third wave" of democratization then roared through Latin America in the 1980s, reached Asian shores later in the decade, and by the early 1990s had swept away communism in Eastern Europe and the former USSR. It was the fall of the Berlin Wall and, two years later, the de-mise of the Soviet Union that truly transformed the world and ushered in a period of global democratic hegemony. The next chapter in this collection, "The Democratic Moment," offers my reflections on the situation and prospects of democracy in the wake of these momentous events.

The democratic resurgence in the realm of ideas lagged behind somewhat and is much more difficult to chart. Certainly, the intellectual defenders of democracy felt embattled and on the defensive until well into the 1980s. Yet even the gloomy 1970s witnessed the rise to prominence of the issue of human rights, as both dissidents in the communist world and victims of Latin American military rule won wide sympathy in the West. In the United

States, the newfound concern with human rights, first given political voice in the Congress, was elevated to a central point of American foreign policy under the presidency of Jimmy Carter.

DEMOCRACY AND HUMAN RIGHTS

Initially, however, the new boldness in asserting support for human rights was not matched by equivalent efforts on behalf of democracy. That step was taken under the presidency of Ronald Reagan. In his historic June 1982 speech to the British parliament, in which he spoke of "the decay of the Soviet experiment" and consigned Marxism-Leninism to the "ash-heap of history," President Reagan noted the bipartisan efforts then underway to "determine how the United States can best contribute as a nation to the global campaign for democracy now gathering force."[4] That speech led to the creation in late 1983 of the National Endowment for Democracy, a nongovernmental but congressionally funded institution that awarded its first grants in 1984.

In the NED's early years, the very idea of democracy promotion remained intensely controversial. To be sure, the NED was founded on the basis of a bipartisan consensus that brought together the Republican and Democratic parties, the AFL-CIO and the U.S. Chamber of Commerce, and the Reagan White House and the Democratic-dominated Congress. (Indeed, Dante Fascell, a longtime leader of House Democrats on international issues, was perhaps the single most influential figure in bringing the Endowment into existence and served as its first chairman.) And the NED could draw on the precedent of the German political party foundations, which had long provided aid to their counterparts abroad and had played a particularly important role in assisting the transitions to democracy in Spain and Portugal. Yet in the United States skepticism was widespread. Some simply feared that taxpayers' money would be frivolously wasted or unproductively expended. Others opposed U.S.-sponsored "meddling" in other countries' internal affairs, especially through a private organization not subject to the ordinary chain of command that binds government agencies.

But fiscal conservatism and isolationism were not the only ideological grounds for hostility to democracy promotion. In fact, some of the sharpest opposition came from those most committed to a vigorous human rights policy. Today the once-sharp split between the "human rights community" and the "democracy community" may seem difficult to comprehend, given the close interrelationship in both theory and practice between human rights and democracy. In part, this rift derived from the accidents of partisan politics in the United States. In the disputes over Central America that roiled American politics in the mid-1980s, many human rights advocates tended to focus chiefly on the abuses of right-wing governments and to be hostile to the policies of President Reagan. Democracy promotion came to be identified by some with the Reagan administration in the same way that human rights had been identified with the Carter administration.

These partisan divisions, however, were largely effaced by the downfall of communism and the end of the Cold War. The Clinton administration, upon taking office in 1993, made "democratic enlargement" one of the pillars of its foreign policy, and it proposed a dramatic increase in the budget of the National Endowment for Democracy. And in a move that symbolized the transcending of the rift between human rights advocates and democracy advocates, it reconstituted the State Department's Bureau of Human Rights and Humanitarian Affairs, which had been established under President Carter, into the Bureau of Democracy, Human Rights, and Labor. This evolution is noted in "The Role of Human Rights," the third chapter in this collection, which was originally written as the entry on "Human Rights" for a new *Encyclopedia of Democracy*. The essential goal of this essay, however, is to present in a clear and compact way the philosophical origins of human rights and their relation to democracy.

There was always something curiously asymmetrical about the rift between the human rights community and the democracy community. At least on the conceptual level, democracy advocates always embraced the cause of human rights. Though they may have been more enthusiastic about the merits of elections than their human rights counterparts, they were never pure majoritarians nor did they doubt the primacy of individual rights. Their argument was that instituting democratic governments was the only reliable way to ensure respect for human rights. Some human rights advocates, by contrast, did seem to doubt the superiority of democratic government—or at least argued that the principle of human rights was wholly independent of political regimes. For them, human rights constituted a universal juridical norm, best affirmed through international standards; thus, to link human rights to a particular kind of political order was to "politicize" them and call into question their universality. These differences are still sometimes visible in debates over the role of international institutions versus democratic nation-states (a subject to which I turn later in this volume), but for most practical purposes the human rights and democracy communities today are strong allies. Whether in Russia, or in Burma, or in Zimbabwe, or in China, or in Uzbekistan, contemporary struggles for human rights are also struggles for democracy.

YEARS OF TRIUMPH

The first half of the 1990s was truly a period of democratic triumph. In 1990, according to Freedom House, the number of democracies in the

world (which had been at 39 in 1974) had still only reached 76, representing well under half of the world's 165 independent countries. But by 1995,
the number of democracies had climbed to 117, constituting more than 60
percent of the world's independent countries (which had expanded to 191
in number, largely thanks to the breakup of the Soviet Union and Yugoslavia). The early 1990s witnessed not only the Soviet collapse but the
seemingly miraculous peaceful demise of the apartheid regime in South
Africa, a number of democratic transitions elsewhere in sub-Saharan Africa,
and significant democratic advances in Asian nations ranging from
Bangladesh, Nepal, and Thailand to Korea and Taiwan.

Perhaps even more dramatic was the leap in democracy's ideological preeminence and global legitimacy. In the inaugural issue of the *Journal of Democracy*, published in January 1990, Larry Diamond and I had noted that
"despite its intrinsic appeal and its recent triumphs, democracy remains
comparatively weak in the realm of political ideas and organization," and
that "in many cases, Third World democrats feel beleaguered and isolated."[5]
By January 1995, in the introduction to the journal's fifth anniversary issue,
we acknowledged that this generally was no longer true, adding that "Western organizations today are providing considerable assistance to democrats
in the developing and postcommunist countries, and worldwide contacts
among democrats have greatly increased."[6] Moreover, citing the increasingly outspoken endorsements of democracy by leading multilateral organizations, we asserted that "today democracy reigns supreme in the ideological sphere."[7]

The new predominance of democracy, both on the ground and in the
minds of men, completely transformed the political atmosphere surrounding democracy promotion. In an amazingly short period of time, it went
from being a subject of bitter controversy to an enterprise in which almost
everyone wanted a piece of the action. Citizens and government officials in
the new democracies were eager to receive "political development assistance," and institutions in the West, ranging from private foundations to
government aid agencies to multilateral organizations, were increasingly eager to provide it. Anti-imperialism and anti-Americanism suddenly seemed
all but invisible, and recipients, especially in the postcommunist countries,
tended to have no qualms about accepting democracy assistance, even if it
came directly from a U.S. government agency.

LIBERALISM VERSUS DEMOCRACY?

Yet even at the height of democratic euphoria, there were signs that it would
not last. In our January 1995 introduction, we noted that "there are worrisome trends as well. As the past half-decade has shown, toppling dictator-

ships is an easier task than building functioning democracies."[8] The consolidation of new democracies was proving more difficult than most observers had expected. Many aspiring third wave democracies, we warned, "seem stuck in a gray area of quasi-democracy, with shaky political institutions and constitutional systems that fail to provide the minimal conditions of democracy: free and fair competition for power, elected civilian control, accountability, representativeness, and legal guarantees for rights of conscience, expression, organization, and assembly."[9] Writing in the *Journal of Democracy* in July 1996, Diamond elaborated upon this analysis. He noted that despite the meteoric rise in Freedom House's count of democracies (countries that choose their leaders in competitive elections), the number of countries Freedom House ranked as "Free" (based on their performance in terms of guaranteeing civil liberties as well as political rights) had been rising much more slowly. The result was that an increasing proportion of the world's democracies were less than free.[10]

Diamond's analysis emphasized the distinction between genuinely *liberal* democracies that protect the rights of their citizens and adhere to the rule of law and merely *electoral* democracies that are deficient in these respects even though they choose their leaders through competitive elections. The practical conclusion that Diamond drew from this divergence was the need to "deepen" new democracies and to make them more liberal. Such deepening and liberalization, he further argued, would make young democracies more valued by their citizens and hence increase their prospects of becoming consolidated.

Diamond's analysis, however, was to be turned in a different direction by one of the most influential articles on democracy to appear over the past two decades. Writing in *Foreign Affairs* in 1997, Fareed Zakaria chronicled what he called "The Rise of Illiberal Democracy."[11] Zakaria characterized illiberal democracy in much the same way as Diamond had electoral democracy—a regime that freely elects its leaders but fails to safeguard the basic rights of individuals and minorities. But whereas Diamond presented the abuses of such regimes as resulting from a *deficit* (or shallowness) of democracy, Zakaria explained them as resulting from an *excess* of democracy. That is, Zakaria radically emphasized the disjunction between the electoral and liberal strands of liberal democracy, arguing that they were increasingly "coming apart" outside the West: "Democracy is flourishing; constitutional liberalism is not."[12] For Zakaria, the term democracy was properly reserved for such majoritarian devices as elections, while the protection of individual rights and adherence to the rule of law belonged under the banner of liberalism. And he saw democracy as a *threat* to liberalism, especially if it were introduced prematurely in the form of elections in countries that lacked a liberal tradition.

Zakaria's article was powerfully written and in many respects cogently argued. My own earlier thinking about the relationship of human rights to democracy had led me to ponder both the theoretical and practical aspects of the issues Zakaria was raising. On the theoretical level, I felt he had performed a useful service in sharply distinguishing the liberal and the democratic strands of liberal democracy. And yet I thought he had overstated the disjunction between the two and drawn from it a set of practical recommendations that were likely to be harmful to the cause of liberal democracy around the world. As a result, I decided to enter the debate myself and composed a response to Zakaria's essay that I submitted to *Foreign Affairs*. As Zakaria was managing editor of *Foreign Affairs* at the time, I appreciate the fair-mindedness and generosity of spirit he displayed in accepting for publication my critique, which appears as the fourth chapter in this volume under the title "The Links between Liberalism and Democracy."

ANCIENTS VERSUS MODERNS

My understanding of the relationship between democracy and liberalism has been powerfully influenced by the study of ancient political theory and practice. Zakaria's label of "illiberal democracy" is not one that any contemporary regimes are proud to claim as their own. It is a way of characterizing contemporary electoral regimes that have failed—whether from inexperience, incompetence, weakness, or bad faith—to protect individual rights and the rule of law. These regimes regularly repeat their commitment to human rights, even as they continue to violate them. The democracies of ancient Greece, however, were genuinely and wholeheartedly illiberal, in the sense that they did not recognize any claims of human rights that citizens could wield against the polity.

The contrast between the ancients and moderns in this respect was most forcefully stated by Benjamin Constant in his classic essay "The Liberty of the Ancients Compared with That of the Moderns."[13] Constant stresses that the moderns understand liberty in terms of the freedom of the individual to do what he likes, subject only to the laws. For the citizens of ancient democracies, by contrast, liberty consisted in exercising directly a share of the self-government of the city: deliberating on questions of war and peace, passing laws, pronouncing judicial verdicts, and the like. But the collective liberty that the ancients enjoyed as citizens was, according to Constant, accompanied by

> the complete subjection of the individual to the authority of the community. . . . All private actions were submitted to a severe surveillance. No importance was given to individual independence, neither in relation to opinions, nor to labor, nor, above all, to religion. The right to choose one's own religious affiliation, a right which we regard as one of the most precious, would have seemed

to the ancients a crime and a sacrilege. . . . Thus among the ancients the individual, almost always sovereign in public affairs, was a slave in all his private relations. As a citizen, he decided on war and peace; as a private individual, he was constrained, watched, and repressed in all his movements; as a member of the collective body, he interrogated, dismissed, condemned, beggared, exiled, or sentenced to death his magistrates and superiors; as a subject of the collective body he could himself be deprived of his status, stripped of his privileges, banished, put to death, by the discretionary will of the whole to which he belonged.[14]

In sum, as Constant put it, "The ancients . . . had no notion of individual rights."[15]

In the ancient democracies personal freedom was sacrificed on the altar of a community of equal citizens. But it is well to remember that ancient notions of equality were quite different from our own, as is reflected in the fact that even in the most democratic polities of Greece, only a small percentage of the inhabitants were citizens, and slavery was practiced on a large scale. The founding philosophers of liberalism—above all, Thomas Hobbes and John Locke—not only introduced the idea of universal human rights but also tied it directly to the concept of the natural equality of all human beings: Men are born not only free but also equal. It is precisely because of their natural equality that no man is entitled to rule another without the latter's consent. While liberalism is indeed in some respects in tension with democracy, as the case of the ancients shows, there is a profound underlying kinship between liberalism and *modern* democracy, a kinship that Zakaria's argument ignores. It is for this reason that the "liberal autocracy" that Zakaria espouses as his preferred alternative to illiberal democracy has virtually disappeared from the contemporary world.

THE DEMOCRATIZATION OF LIBERALISM

The absence of liberal autocracies today is in part due to the fact that the liberal autocracies of previous eras have now all evolved into liberal democracies. My effort to grasp the dynamic that drove this evolution, initiated in my response to Zakaria, is explored in greater detail in the fifth chapter in this collection, "Why Liberalism Became Democratic." It shows that the fears expressed by Zakaria—that democracy poses a threat to liberalism— were widely voiced in the nineteenth century. Thinkers such as the eminent British historian Lord Macaulay argued that the extension of the franchise to the poor would spell the doom of the rights of property on which a liberal order depends. Other thinkers, however, most notably Tocqueville, foresaw both that the extension of the franchise was inevitable and that it would *not* lead to the plunder of the rich or to economic decline. Judging in part on the basis of nineteenth-century America, Tocqueville correctly concluded that democracy need not undermine liberalism, and that liberal democracy might well represent the wave of the future.

Zakaria's article provoked an intense debate that continues to this day, largely in the form of disputes over the best way to encourage the growth of liberal democracy. Zakaria and others in his camp, including Jack Snyder and Edward Mansfield and Amy Chua, have stressed the danger of premature elections and the threat posed to the freedom of individuals and minorities by popular majorities.[16] Thus they have favored democracy-promotion strategies that aim at securing the rule of law, property rights, and constitutional restraints before opening up a political system to electoral choice. In January 2007 Thomas Carothers wrote a powerful critique of the wisdom and practicality of this approach, which he dubbed "The 'Sequencing' Fallacy."[17] But in light of the recent setbacks to democracy promotion in Iraq and elsewhere, there is no doubt that this debate will continue.

At the same time, there was surprisingly little opposition to Zakaria's exalting of liberal constitutionalism over popular rule. Today "populism" has largely become a term of opprobrium (though much less so in the United States than elsewhere), and one meets with very few arguments for giving popular majorities a more direct sway over public policy. Nor is this just a view held by elites. Opinion polls show that almost everywhere the people's trust in their own elected representatives is low, while they tend to have greater confidence in institutions that are less directly responsive to the public. Indeed, the trend in new democracies has been to give greater power to unelected courts and other autonomous agencies (like central banks or independent electoral commissions), and not to have more frequent recourse to the voice of the people. But if liberalism reigns triumphant, so too do the principles of universal inclusion and of the ultimate sovereignty of the people, principles that Zakaria himself does not dispute. For the most part, the concerns expressed have not been about the desirability or the viability of liberal democracy itself; they have centered around the proper balance between its liberal and its democratic features, and the best strategy for bringing both into being.

THE CHALLENGE OF GLOBALIZATION

By the latter half of the 1990s, the global advance of democracy had begun to slow. General Pervez Musharraf's coup in Pakistan in 1999 marked the first sudden and unambiguous reversion to authoritarianism in a major new democracy, prompting fears that what Huntington had called a "reverse wave" of democratization might be in the offing. Yet on the whole, global momentum remained on the side of democracy. Dictatorial rule was brought to an end in key regional powers Indonesia and Nigeria, and democratically minded opposition parties came to power in Croatia, Slovakia, and Serbia in the postcommunist world, as well as in Korea, Taiwan, Mexico, Senegal, and Ghana. And in the absence of powerful ideological alternatives, the global prestige and legitimacy of democracy rose even higher. But a new potential challenge emerged on the horizon—that of globalization.

In the years leading up to the beginning of the new millennium, the word and the concept of globalization were being invoked almost everywhere. The combination of increasingly open global markets and startling advances in communications technology—symbolized by the Internet—seemed to be transforming not only the world economy but the international political landscape as well. The most confident and visionary thinkers and publicists of this otherwise largely nonideological period were the enthusiasts of the Internet and of a globalized economy, who hailed the beginnings of a new cosmopolitan political order in which national borders would largely lose their relevance. Meanwhile, a heterogeneous "antiglobalization" movement, which achieved a high level of visibility through protests against the World Bank and the IMF, tried to take advantage of popular fears over the dislocations caused by the globalization of the economy. Those on both sides of this debate tended to see themselves as supporters rather than opponents of democracy. The complex relationship between globalization and democracy is the topic of the sixth chapter in this collection, entitled "Globalization and Self-Government."

In thinking through the implications of globalization for the future of democracy, I found it very helpful to draw upon the basic analysis that had informed my earlier essays exploring the tensions, as well as the complementarities, between the liberal and the democratic strands of liberal democracy. For with regard to globalization, these two elements of liberal democracy seem to point in opposite directions. The liberal component has a universal character, as it is derived from the rights equally shared by all human beings. Liberalism limits the power and reach of government in the name of individual rights. In principle, it would be readily compatible with a single universal world state as opposed to separate nations. Since all human beings are entitled to the same rights, there is no strictly liberal reason why they should be divided by arbitrary political borders or have a variety of governments entrusted with protecting their rights.

The democratic or self-governing aspect of liberal democracy, however, requires that the people choose their governors and hold them accountable. This means that the people must have particular ties that bind them to one another as members of the same political community. They must be not just possessors of human rights but citizens with a special attachment to their fellow countrymen. This in turn demands a certain sense of kinship

that is not easily fostered among individuals who are separated by profound linguistic, cultural, and historical differences. On the scale of a world
state, in fact, cultivating the requisite sense of kinship or citizenship would
surely be impossible.

THE U.S. VERSUS THE EU

"Globalization and Self-Government" concludes with a brief comparison of
the United States and the European Union, focusing on their differing responses to the issues posed by globalization and their contrasting approaches to combining liberalism with self-government. This is a subject I
explore in greater depth in the three essays that follow. During the early years
of the new century, the transatlantic rift that separated America from many
of its longtime European allies dominated discussions of international politics. The European Union, as it moved simultaneously toward expansion to
include the postcommunist countries of Central Europe and toward the
adoption of a constitution, was regarded by many observers as offering a
new political model superior to that of the United States (or other individual nation-states). At the height of the debate over European-American relations and the future of the European Union, I spent the 2002–2003 academic year studying these questions as a visiting professor at the Robert
Schuman Centre of the European University Institute in Florence.

There I tried to understand the European Union, a highly complex and
often mystifying institution. This task was made more difficult by the fact
that discussion of the EU has developed its own specialized vocabulary,
which is often hard for outsiders to penetrate. But even after getting beyond
the terminological hurdles, one encounters the fact that people with different political perspectives, as well as academic specialists, sharply disagree
about what the EU's goals are and exactly what kind of thing it is. This is
due not simply to the institution's complexity, but also to the studied ambiguity that the EU has maintained about the final end toward which it is
heading—an ambiguity that helped it to retain support as it gradually increased its reach and its scope. The seventh chapter in this collection, "Understanding the European Union," seeks to provide readers with basic
knowledge about the evolution and structure of the EU but also to explore
the competing and often conflicting opinions about its real nature.

The traditional ways of viewing the EU had been rooted in the study either of federalism or of international organizations: Is the EU an intergovernmental organization like the UN or the Organization of American States,
where individual states remain sovereign but cooperate in pursuit of common interests? Or is it an embryonic federal polity, where the central government enjoys ultimate sovereignty over the individual states? There is ev-

idence to support both propositions, as the EU seems to have much more authority over its member states than an international organization does, but much less authority than a federal government has over its constituent units. Increasingly, however, leading scholars who study the European Union have come to reject either pole of this argument. They argue that the EU should not be understood as occupying some point along the line that stretches between an intergovernmental organization and a federal state, but exists on a different plane altogether.

This is where the issue of globalization comes in. For these scholars assert that in an era of globalization old models and concepts of state sovereignty will no longer do. The nation-state, which has reigned supreme since the Peace of Westphalia in 1648, is entering its obsolescence, and new models of political organization ("post-Westphalian," "postnational," or "postmodern") need to be created. In this new era, traditional notions of sovereignty are losing their relevance, and it would be short-sighted to try to capture the character of the EU using such outmoded categories. According to this way of looking at things, the EU, even though it is a regional body, is the harbinger of the new political forms that will come to the fore in a globalized world.

DEMOCRACY AND THE NATION-STATE

A more theoretical exploration of the "postmodern" approach to the issue of sovereignty—and its implications for democracy—is offered in the essay that follows, entitled "Sovereignty and Democracy." Although democracy tends not to be a central issue for postmodern theorists of the EU, most of them would certainly not identify themselves as opponents of democracy. They are, however, outspoken in their hostility to the nation-state—or at least to the position it occupies as the central ordering principle of political life throughout the world. But since modern liberal democracy has emerged and flourished only within the framework of the nation-state, this poses the question of whether that framework can be abandoned without sacrificing its progeny.

Proponents of the postmodern view, such as international relations scholar John Ruggie, regard the nation-state as a historically contingent and morally questionable institution whose time is passing. Ruggie asserts that the international order existing since the Peace of Westphalia, based upon "territorially defined, fixed and mutually exclusive enclaves of legitimate domination . . . appears to be unique in human history."[18] In his view, Europe in the age of feudalism, with its competing and overlapping claims to sovereignty, is closer to the historical norm and a more likely guide to the political patterns of the future. I argue that this is dubious as history (most obviously, it neglects the city-states of antiquity), and that it also fails to take account of the link between territorially defined and mutually exclusive political entities and the possibility of self-government.

It is one thing for empires or other political forms in which rulers are not accountable to their subjects to have vague boundaries or unclear lines of jurisdiction. But if citizens are to be agents of self-government, it must be clear who is a citizen and how far the sway of the citizenry extends. As political scientists Juan Linz and Alfred Stepan put it, "Without a state, there can be no citizenship; without citizenship, there can be no democracy."[19] This is a problem that proponents of the postmodern approach have not sufficiently considered. The recurring complaints that the EU suffers from a "democratic deficit," widely acknowledged to be valid (not least in official proclamations of the EU itself), underline the seriousness of this problem. If there is no clear locus or demarcation of sovereignty, it is hard to see how the people can be sovereign. The question of whether a "non-state" political order can be made compatible with citizenship and the accountability of rulers remains unresolved, and should present a warning flag to those theorists who enthusiastically foresee the obsolescence of the nation-state. For abandoning or diluting the concept of sovereignty may entail abandoning government by and responsive to the people.

INTERNATIONALISM

Although some analysts have seen the rift between the United States and the European Union as connected with their differences regarding the desirability of promoting democracy around the world, the Europeans have been much more favorably disposed to democracy promotion than many realize. Both the EU and its member states have launched their own programs of democracy assistance, and there is frequently smooth cooperation between Americans and Europeans in aiding democratic forces in particular developing or postcommunist countries. Moreover, in their recent public pronouncements the Europeans have been surprisingly willing to endorse democracy promotion as a key goal of foreign policy. In discussions between Americans and Europeans about democracy promotion, significant differences rarely emerge at the level of values or principles. The real divergences are over means, and the discussions turn truly contentious only when they move to such questions as the role of international law or the use of force. The heart of the dispute often centers around the relative merits of multilateral versus unilateral approaches to foreign policy issues. This question is the starting point for the next essay in this volume, "Two Kinds of Internationalism."

In my view, the split that has developed between the United States and many of its allies on this point derives less from changes in the U.S. approach than from a shift in the way multilateralism has come to be understood. Traditional "liberal internationalism" was based on the principle of national sovereignty, as the Charter of the United Nations (and indeed, the organization's very name) makes plain. In recent years, however, multilateralism has in large part been redefined to transcend the old internationalism in the name of a new "globalism." This globalist perspective stresses that, in today's highly interconnected world, the gravest threats to peace may arise not from interstate relations but from such problems as environmental degradation, terrorism, disease, and international criminal networks. Since the scale of the challenges confronting us is increasingly global, it is said that we must build institutions of "global governance" capable of responding to them.

An extreme formulation of the globalist perspective has been offered by political theorist Benjamin Barber, who asserts that today's "democratic project is to globalize democracy."[20] In Barber's view, "The [American] Declaration of Independence . . . has achieved its task of nation-building. To build the new world that is now required calls for a new Declaration of Interdependence, a declaration recognizing the interdependence of a human race that can no longer survive in fragments—whether the pieces are called nations or tribes, peoples or markets."[21] Once again, the issue posed is whether democracy can transcend the nation, and I explore it by going back to the Declaration of 1776 and the relationship that it posits between the universal principles of human rights and the requirements of national self-government.

Underlying the doctrine of the Declaration is the political philosophy of John Locke, to which I find myself having recourse throughout this volume. In an intensive analysis of Locke's *Second Treatise*, I attempt to illuminate the peculiar combination of the universal and the particular that informs liberal democracy, especially in its American incarnation, and that drives the behavior of the United States in the international arena. For I believe that the internationalist, outward-looking, and universalist aspects of America's outlook on the world are, paradoxically, linked to the factors that make it so jealous of its own political sovereignty, and hence so resistant to the new brand of multilateralism represented by globalism. Even if the globalists are right in their analysis of the problems, their proposed solution risks undermining the foundations of liberal democracy. International cooperation is indeed more needed than ever before, but it must be carried out in a manner that is safe for democracy.

SOBERING EXPERIENCES

Though the underlying forces of globalization remain at work, it soon became apparent that they would not quickly transform the harsh realm of international politics. The Internet facilitated communication among democrats but also among terrorists and their supporters. In any case, it did not notably undermine the power of governments or make national borders irrelevant. As for the European Union, it suffered a severe setback in 2005 when voters in both France and the Netherlands rejected the proposed new constitution. As European leaders called for a "period of reflection," popular opposition to admitting new member states seemed to be on the rise. Meanwhile, transatlantic disagreements became less sharp and less preoccupying, as other concerns came to the fore.

Regarding the state of democracy, there emerged a growing pessimism. In an introduction to the *Journal of Democracy*'s fifteenth anniversary issue in January 2005, I began by noting that "the mood among supporters of democracy is perhaps more somber than it has been since we began," and cited three recent political developments that had contributed to the gloom: (1) the difficulties of democracy building in Iraq, (2) the regression to authoritarianism in Russia, and (3) the global rise of anti-Americanism, which, because of the widespread identification of democracy and democracy promotion with the United States, tended to cast the entire enterprise in question.[22]

The gloom was briefly lifted, however, by a remarkable series of events in late 2004 and in 2005. As the journal's fifteenth anniversary issue was in press, Ukraine was successfully carrying out its Orange Revolution. Not only was this a heartening development in itself, but it seemed to spark a new wave of prodemocratic upheavals. In March of 2005, Kyrgyz autocrat Askar Akayev was ousted by popular demonstrations, seemingly indicating that "color revolutions" could succeed in the Asian as well as European parts of the former Soviet Union.

Other dramatic developments unfolded in the Middle East. In January 2005, Palestinians were given an opportunity to vote in presidential elections for the first time since 1996 and elected Mahmoud Abbas as president of the Palestinian authority. Later that same month the world witnessed the vivid expressions of joy by Iraqis who braved dangerous security conditions to vote in elections for their transitional National Assembly. These electoral contests in the Arab world and Ukraine's Orange Revolution both contributed to inspiring the Cedar Revolution in Lebanon. There massive demonstrations sparked by the February 2005 assassination of ex-premier Rafik Hariri led, within a few months, to the withdrawal of Syrian troops and a victory by prodemocratic forces in parliamentary elections. With President Mubarak agreeing to liberalize the conditions for Egypt's presidential elections scheduled for later that year, high hopes arose that real democratic progress might at last be coming to the Middle East.

Unfortunately, by early 2007 most of these hopes had been dashed. In Iraq, despite two additional successful electoral exercises, the victorious parties were all communally based, and the new government proved unable to stop growing sectarian violence. Egypt's 2005 elections were far from impartial, and the only opposition forces to gain were those of the Islamist Muslim Brotherhood. In the Palestinian territories, legislative elections in January 2006 were conducted fairly but resulted in a victory for Hamas, an Islamist party that refused to renounce violence. In Iran, voters gave a second-round victory in presidential elections to hard-liner Mahmoud Ahmadinejad, ensuring that this country, which many observers had believed was ripe for democratization, would remain a leader of antidemocratic forces in the region. With Iranian support, Hezbollah in Lebanon was able to provoke and then to withstand a 2006 war with Israel, which enflamed the Middle East and supplanted the reformist discourse that had been growing there with the old slogans of Arab hostility to Israel and the United States. Meanwhile, democratic progress slowed or stalled in the "color revolution" countries of Ukraine, Kyrgyzstan, and Lebanon, and authoritarian tendencies grew stronger in Russia and in most of the other ex-Soviet states. And toward the end of 2006 successful coups were mounted in Thailand and Fiji.

The latter half of 2005 and 2006 also saw the rise of a new assault on democracy promotion. Assistance to democrats in developing and postcommunist countries had been growing in magnitude and international legitimacy throughout the post-Cold War period. Even the terrorist attacks of September 11, 2001, which might have been expected to result (at least in the United States) in a narrowing focus on "hard-power" instruments of national security, had not been able to slow the progress of democracy assistance. In fact, 9/11 had the opposite effect, with the U.S. Congress becoming more receptive to funding democracy programs and the Bush administration coming to identify support for democratization as a key weapon in the war on terror, elevating it to the centerpiece of U.S. foreign policy. The new visibility that this brought proved to be a mixed blessing, however. In the minds of many opponents of the Iraq war around the globe, democracy assistance came to be conflated with the use of military force to achieve "regime change." More generally, the global rise of anti-Americanism supplied a receptive audience for those claiming that democracy assistance was just part of a U.S. plot to achieve "global hegemony."

At the same time, the success of the "color revolutions" threw fear into the hearts of authoritarian rulers, especially those in so-called "hybrid regimes" (regimes that permit multiparty elections but try to manipulate them in favor of incumbents). These rulers concluded that external assistance had been critical to the success of popular protests in overturning the results of rigged elections, and determined to forestall similar occurrences in their own domains. As a result, in such countries as Russia, Venezuela, Zimbabwe, Belarus, and Egypt, new efforts were made to restrict the activities of local and international NGOs and to place obstacles in the way of democracy assistance from abroad. The imposition of these measures must also be viewed in the context of a broader global trend—rising self-confidence and increased cooperation on the part of nondemocratic regimes (many of them bolstered by soaring oil revenues) united by their opposition to democracy, human rights, and U.S. foreign policy.

Thus, by 2007 democracy and the effort to promote it were facing greater challenges than at any period since the end of the Cold War. Yet many powerful assets remained on the side of the world's democrats, not least among them the absence of any ideological competitors whose doctrines can command broad worldwide appeal. However tarnished liberal democracy might appear in the eyes of some, it retains unrivaled global legitimacy and prestige. What does all this portend for the future of democracy around the world? That is the question to which I devote the concluding chapter, "The Democratic Moment Revisited," which seeks both to review the forecasts made in the 1991 essay that appears as the following chapter in this book and to speculate about how democracy's fortunes may evolve in the years to come.

2

The Democratic Moment

1991

The dramatic events of August 1991 in Moscow should convince any remaining skeptics that the democratic revolutions of 1989 indeed marked a watershed in world history. The sudden downfall that year of long-entrenched communist regimes throughout Eastern Europe dramatically transformed the face of world politics. Together with the remarkable changes that had already taken place in both the foreign and domestic policies of the Soviet Union, this development effectively brought to an end the period, beginning in 1945, that has generally been labeled the postwar or Cold War era. Yet despite the general consensus that we have now entered the post–Cold War era, there is sharp disagreement about what the nature and characteristics of this new period will be.

Before addressing this central question, it is worth briefly reviewing the Cold War era and the dynamics that brought it to a close. In the years following the Second World War, the militarily strongest and economically most advanced nations of the world became divided into two sharply opposed camps headed by two superpowers, the United States and the Soviet Union. The division of the world into East and West was marked by the "Iron Curtain" that ran through the middle of Germany and the heart of Central Europe. But the split between East and West was not only geopolitical; it was also a conflict between two fundamentally opposed ideologies— Leninist communism and liberal democracy. Many countries sought to maintain varying degrees of neutrality in this struggle, styling themselves as the Nonaligned Movement or the Third World, but they remained more an arena for superpower competition than a potent independent force in global politics. It is hard to quarrel with the characterization of the international system during the Cold War era as a bipolar world.

Although there was great immobility in this system from 1949 on, the changes that did take place generally seemed to strengthen the Soviet camp. It is now apparent to almost everyone that the communist regimes had long been disintegrating from within, but during most of the Cold War period communism seemed to be enjoying a slow but steady ascendancy. It gradually brought a number of additional non-European countries into its orbit; during the 1970s alone, new procommunist regimes emerged in some dozen nations. Even more significant was the seeming irreversibility of such gains. In fact, until the U.S. intervention in Grenada in 1983, not a single consolidated communist regime had ever been displaced.

Meanwhile, democracy, after receiving a brief ideological boost from the establishment of new democratic regimes during the wave of decolonization, seemed to be in deep trouble. The postcolonial democracies almost all soon failed, giving way to regimes that were authoritarian and generally "nonaligned," though with a strong admixture of hostility toward the West. The imposition of dictatorial rule in India by Indira Gandhi in 1975, seemingly bringing to an end the largest and most important democracy in the non-Western world, marked a low point for democratic fortunes. At that very moment, Daniel Patrick Moynihan, a staunch champion of liberal democracy, despairingly wrote:

> Liberal democracy on the American model increasingly tends to the condition of monarchy in the nineteenth century: a holdover form of government, one which persists in isolated or peculiar places here and there, and may even serve well enough for special circumstances, but which has simply no relevance to the future. It is where the world was, not where it is going.[1]

Although the late 1970s witnessed transitions to democracy in Spain and Portugal and its restoration in India, only in the 1980s did it become clear that Moynihan's pessimism was unfounded and that democracy was experiencing a true resurgence. The democratic tide swept through most of Latin America, reached such key Asian countries as the Philippines, Korea, Taiwan, and Pakistan, and by decade's end was beginning to make ripples in sub-Saharan Africa and even the Middle East. Moreover, the 1980s saw such Third World alternatives to democracy as African socialism and bureaucratic authoritarianism in Latin America revealed as political and economic failures.

Most dramatic, of course, was the growing crisis—and in some places the sudden collapse—of communism. Not only did the 1980s witness no new communist gains, but existing communist regimes were suddenly thrown on the defensive. Relatively new pro-Soviet regimes were challenged by U.S.-backed anticommunist insurgencies in Afghanistan, Angola, and Nicaragua. Yet while these armed resistance movements may have taken a physical, economic, and psychological toll on communist governments, it is noteworthy that so far they have nowhere come to power. Except for the cases of Romania and of Ethiopia (where the victorious insurgent movements were Marxist in origin), Eastern European and Third World communist regimes have ceded power largely through negotiations, elections, and other peaceful means.

This peaceful denouement was made possible, of course, by the internal crisis of communism at its very core in the Soviet Union. We are still very far from having an adequate understanding of how this once seemingly impregnable regime could crumble so quickly, or of the motives and strategies of the chief architect of its undoing, Mikhail Gorbachev. What does seem clear is that by the 1980s, Soviet communism faced a choice between continuing socioeconomic stagnation and reform. But modest reform proved incapable of overcoming stagnation, and more thoroughgoing reform proved impossible without decisively undermining the communist system. In the formulation of one of communism's most acute analysts, the Yugoslav dissident Milovan Djilas, the liberalization of communism turned out to be identical with the crisis of communism.

Even more damaging to communism than its economic failures and foreign policy reverses was its ideological self-discrediting. By attributing their system's shortcomings to its lack of economic markets and political democracy, the Soviet leaders effectively conceded the ideological struggle to the West and dealt communism's worldwide appeal a mortal blow. Who wants to devote oneself to a cause that has been repudiated by its own most prominent spokesmen? Today's international political heroes are no longer leftist revolutionaries, but the peaceful protesters demanding democracy who were so brutally crushed in Tiananmen Square or who triumphed in Wenceslas Square (and, most recently, at the barricades surrounding the Russian Parliament). In this context, let us also note what may be viewed as a coda to the revolutions of 1989: the peaceful rejection of the Sandinistas at the polls by the people of Nicaragua, which ended the last pro-Soviet Third World regime still capable of eliciting passionate support in the West.

THE POST-COLD WAR WORLD

We thus find ourselves living in the new post–Cold War world—a world with one dominant principle of political legitimacy, democracy, and only one superpower, the United States. But how long can this, the democratic moment, last? Is democracy's unchallenged preeminence, with no serious geopolitical or ideological rivals, only transitory, a momentary worldwide "era of good feelings" that will soon give way to bitter new divisions? Or does it signal a lasting victory due either to democracy's own inherent strengths or to the shortcomings of antidemocratic regimes and ideologies?

The most forceful statement of the latter view, of course, is to be found in Francis Fukuyama's now famous article "The End of History?" where he asserts that we may be witnessing "the end point of man's ideological evolution and the universalization of Western liberal democracy as the final form of human government." While there is reason to be dubious about the metaphysical trappings and sweeping conclusions of Fukuyama's thesis, he was absolutely right with respect to what may be considered the essential premise of his essay—namely, "the total exhaustion of viable systematic alternatives to Western liberalism."[2]

The collapse of communism and the manifest failure of various authoritarian brands of Third Worldism have resulted in the absence of a single nondemocratic regime in the world with wide appeal. They have also led to a drastic weakening of openly antidemocratic forces within democratic regimes. Just as the defeat of fascism led to the virtual disappearance of the antidemocratic right in the West, so the downfall of communism seems to be causing the withering away of the antidemocratic left.

Moreover, it is not solely the extreme or antidemocratic left that has suffered from the crisis of "really existing socialism." For example, Miklós Haraszti, a former underground writer who is now a member of the Hungarian parliament, describes the current political spectrum in his country as follows:

> All in all what we have here is a quite classic European feature: a conservative and liberal side to modern society, where in conformity with the political reality of postcommunist democracy there is no left as such. . . . In postcommunist societies, you see, the left is dead. . . . So the structure we have now is an American kind of political split, and in that sense East European politics is closer to the U.S. rather than the West European model.[3]

Yet to some extent the development Haraszti describes in Eastern Europe can also be observed in Western Europe (and even Latin America), as socialist parties continue to move toward the center.[4] Without too much exaggeration, one might say that today there is no Left left. Everywhere in the more advanced countries, politics is tending to move closer to the U.S. model—not only in being influenced by American campaign and media techniques, but in the more important respect of being dominated by moderate center-left and center-right parties united in agreement on fundamental democratic principles and procedures, and increasingly on an acceptance of the market economy as well.

Even before the collapse of communism, the 1980s had witnessed a remarkable rehabilitation of free-market economics in the West. Not only had capitalism gained a new intellectual respectability, but the successful entrepreneur once again became an object of admiration. By contrast, state ownership of the means of production came to be identified not with economic progress but with stagnation. The eagerness of communist and especially postcommunist countries to transform themselves into market economies dramatically reinforced this trend.

The discrediting of traditional socialist economics contributed significantly to restoring the self-confidence of liberal democracy. It helped bring to an end a long-established tendency in the West to view modern democracy as moving "progressively" in the direction of an ever greater role for the state, and even to see socialism as the logical culmination of liberal democracy. From this perspective, no matter how retrograde communist states may have seemed with respect to their denial of civil and political liberties, they nonetheless had some claim to be more "modern," to represent the wave of the future. The evidence and testimony that have recently emerged from Eastern Europe and the Soviet Union have utterly undermined this way of thinking.

REJOINING WORLD CIVILIZATION

Indeed, today it is the liberal democracies that are widely regarded as the only truly and fully modern societies. This sentiment is reflected in the often expressed desire on the part of Soviets and Eastern Europeans to live in a "normal society." It is a sentiment that was shared not only by dissident intellectuals but also by many representatives of the ruling elites—especially by those who had traveled abroad—and it played a critical role in the demise of communist regimes.

These regimes founded their legitimacy on an ideology that claimed that its adherents constituted the vanguard of a new world. Yet the people living under these regimes came to realize that they were drifting into backwardness and stagnation, that the world was passing them by, that they were laboring under what Milan Šimečka called "the burden of wasted time."[5] In a speech to the Russian parliament, Boris Yeltsin blamed the socialist experiment for leaving the people of the Soviet Union "at the tail end of world civilization."[6]

When they speak of rejoining world civilization, Soviets and Eastern Europeans mean that they want to return to "Europe"—to a market economy and to political democracy. Václav Klaus, the finance minister of Czechoslovakia and the elected leader of Civic Forum, recently stated in answer to a question about his country's economic policies: "We are absolutely not interested in a 'third way' solution. I believe that 'the third way' is the fastest way to the Third World."[7] Many others, both in the West and in the Third World itself, have now come to identify statist economies and nondemocratic polities with corruption and retrogression. Third World intellectuals whose greatest worry once was that their countries would be dominated by

Western capital now voice the fear that Latin America or Africa will become "marginalized" from the world economy.

It is true, of course, that not all nondemocratic Third World regimes have been economic failures. In fact, some authoritarian regimes with relatively open, market-oriented economies—Taiwan, Korea, Chile—have achieved extraordinary economic success. Yet that very success, by fostering and augmenting the power of a self-reliant and outward-looking middle class, has raised popular demands for democratic government that have led to significant political transformations in all of these countries. Authoritarian rulers in developing countries seem to face a kind of catch-22: They are undermined by both economic failure and economic success.

These economically successful Third World authoritarian regimes have held some attraction for certain communist reformers. This has led to the curious spectacle of Taiwan becoming a model in some quarters in Beijing and Pinochet becoming a hero in some quarters in Moscow. The arguments of many of those in both countries attracted by this "neoauthoritarian" model are similar: The premature introduction of political democracy, they assert, will allow popular opposition to forestall the painful measures necessary to introduce a market economy. A strong hand, à la Pinochet, is needed to implement the economic reforms, which will in turn lay the basis for the gradual transition to democracy. It is interesting to note that the strongest argument in favor of authoritarianism today is its alleged ability to dismantle a socialist economy. But even this neoauthoritarian doctrine seems to acknowledge the ultimate superiority of liberal democracy as the eventual goal toward which it aims.

While there may be room for debate about the relative capacity of democracies and market-oriented authoritarian regimes to achieve economic growth in developing countries, only democracy seems compatible with economic success in the advanced nations. Soviet-style command economies may have achieved substantial gains at an earlier phase of industrialization, but building more and bigger steel mills is no longer the measure of economic progress. In the era of computers and instant worldwide telecommunications, innovation, adaptability, and openness to the world economy are essential to maintaining economic competitiveness. And it is difficult for these characteristics to persist for long where political freedom is seriously curtailed.

Democracies also appear to enjoy a comparable advantage with respect to military power. Despite their generally pacific character, they are more capable of producing and operating the weapons that are essential to victory on the battlefield. As Adam Smith had already observed two centuries ago: "In modern war the great expense of firearms gives an evident advantage to the nation which can best afford that expense."[8] Today, as the war against Iraq has underlined, technological superiority is as essential as the ability to equip, deploy, and maintain a large force in the field. It would be rash, given the evidence of past Nazi and Soviet military achievements, to be overconfident about the inability of totalitarian powers to compete militarily with democracies. Yet it does seem that a growing sense of being unable to keep pace economically and technologically in their military competition with the United States was crucial in persuading the Soviet elite to embark on the path of reform.

Democracy seems, then, to enjoy superiority not merely in popular legitimacy and ideological appeal, but also in economic and military strength. And it is difficult to discern any powerful new nondemocratic ideological, economic, or military challengers on the horizon. All this would appear to suggest that, if we have not yet arrived at Fukuyama's "end of history," we may at least be entering a sustained period of peaceful democratic hegemony—a kind of "Pax Democratica."

A NEW IDEOLOGY?

Perhaps the most compelling counterargument to this view of democracy triumphant has been presented by Ken Jowitt.[9] Although writing in explicit opposition to Fukuyama, Jowitt agrees with him that the collapse of communism has resulted in a situation where "liberal capitalism is now the only politically global civilization." For Jowitt, however, this is only an initial and temporary effect of what he calls "the Leninist extinction." He argues that the sudden demise of one of the two camps long engaged in a comprehensive global struggle will lead not to the easy and unchallenged ascendancy of its rival but to a radical reshaping of all the previously fixed boundaries of international politics.

In the first place, this refers to the territorial borders that separate sovereign states. The Leninist extinction not only has fostered the breakup of the Soviet Union but is likely to unleash more open ethnic conflict and the redrawing of national borders among peoples who were previously restrained by Soviet imperial power. There is ample historical precedent for believing that the breakup of empires can lead to new eruptions of long-dormant conflicts between previously subject peoples. Brian Urquhart, who served for several decades as UN undersecretary general for special political affairs, has said that most of his professional life was spent dealing with the problems that the British Empire left in its wake—the Arab-Israeli conflict, the Indo-Pakistani conflict, the Nigerian civil war, the Cyprus dispute. (If Urquhart had stayed on the job a bit longer, he could have added the Iraq-Kuwait conflict to the list.) It would not be surprising if UN officials in the decades ahead were to find themselves similarly preoccupied with crises arising from conflicts between Armenians and Azeris, Hungarians and Romanians, or Croats and Serbs.

But Jowitt argues that the disorder spawned by the Leninist extinction will not be confined to the peoples who once lived under the Leninist yoke. During the Cold War, the superpowers' influence over their client states and their fear of a wider conflict helped to maintain the territorial status quo. Today superpower rivalry is much diminished as a source of Third World conflict, but by the same token it no longer serves to restrain the ambitions of local rulers. Saddam Hussein's invasion of Kuwait is a dramatic example of how the diminution of Soviet power might lead to new regional instability. To be sure, Saddam's expulsion from Kuwait has sent a most salutary message to Third World dictators contemplating territorial aggression. Yet there is reason to doubt that the West would respond so resolutely to aggression in a strategically less critical area of the world.

Jowitt's argument goes beyond asserting that the Leninist extinction will lead to an increase in local wars and a redrawing of territorial boundaries. For he asserts that the vacuum left behind by the "clearing away" of communism may well be filled by the emergence of new ideologies. Liberal democracy, he argues, cannot hold the field to itself because, in "its elevation of rational impersonality as the organizing principle of social life," it fails to satisfy certain basic human longings. Therefore, the West, in his words, "will regularly witness the rise of both internal and external movements dedicated to destroying or reforming it—movements that in one form or another will stress ideals of group membership, expressive behavior, collective solidarity, and heroic action."

Fukuyama might actually agree with a surprisingly large part of Jowitt's argument. For far from predicting the end of international conflict, Fukuyama envisages "a high and perhaps rising level of ethnic and nationalist violence," as well as the continuation of terrorism and wars of national liberation. Nor would he necessarily dispute Jowitt's prediction that we will see the emergence of what the latter calls "movements of rage" in the Third World—"nihilistic backlashes" against political and economic failure such as are embodied in groups like the Khmer Rouge or Peru's Sendero Luminoso. In a sense Fukuyama responds in advance to possible developments of this kind by stating: "Our task is not to answer exhaustively the challenges to liberalism promoted by every crackpot messiah around the world, but only those that are embodied in important social or political forces and movements, and which are therefore part of world history."

This finally brings us to the heart of the disagreement between these two authors. Fukuyama seems to contend that the liberal democratic idea has definitively triumphed among the advanced nations of the world, and thus that there will not again arise a major power animated by an antidemocratic ideology. Jowitt, by contrast, can envisage the emergence of a new ideology capable of generating a new "way of life"—an ideology whose power to move great nations would be comparable to that of Catholicism, liberal democracy, fascism, or Leninism.

Of course, one can only speculate about whether a potent and attractive new ideology will emerge to challenge democracy. Fukuyama persuasively points to the widespread appeal of liberal democracy, its ability to penetrate diverse cultures and win adherents around the world, and the absence of plausible contenders to dethrone it from its current hegemony. Much less convincing, however, is his suggestion that modern liberalism has resolved all the fundamental "contradictions" in human life. As Jowitt argues, liberalism will always leave many human beings unsatisfied and hence will generate powerful antiliberal movements. The real question is whether any such movement can succeed in attaining the economic success and broad appeal necessary to compete successfully with liberalism. The answer, which only the future can reveal, will be decisive for the fate of democracy.

CHALLENGES AND COMPETITORS

Despite its broad popular appeal, democracy is not an easy form of government to maintain, especially in poorer countries that lack an educated populace, a substantial middle class, and a democratic culture. The events of the past decade and a half may have exploded the view that democracy can be sustained only in rich Western countries, but they should not give rise to an unwarranted optimism that expects democracy to be quickly achieved and uninterruptedly preserved throughout the world.

It is remarkable how few breakdowns of democracy there have been in the past few years, even under conditions as adverse as those in Peru or the Philippines. Some of the countries that have more recently installed freely elected governments—Nicaragua, Haiti, and Benin, for example—face still more daunting challenges in trying to create stable democratic institutions. Even the formerly communist countries, despite their European heritage and relatively higher levels of economic development, confront an enormously difficult task in seeking simultaneously to introduce market economies and to consolidate democratic political systems. All these experiments currently benefit both from the extraordinary worldwide momentum and prestige of democracy and from still vivid memories of the tyrannical and unsuccessful regimes that they supplanted. Yet as these memories fade and the new democracies encounter the inevitable difficulties that lie ahead, it is only to be expected that some of them will sink back into authoritarianism.

Such backsliding would undoubtedly be a great misfortune for the people of these countries, and it could very easily create some serious economic and foreign policy problems for the established democracies. Yet its impact on the overall fortunes of democracy in the world would not be all that great, so long as no weighty new ideological rival to democracy appears on the scene. If the majority of the new democracies fail and revert to various local brands of authoritarianism, the view might once again become current that democracy is an unworkable or inappropriate system for developing countries, but the presumption would remain that it is the only form of government suitable for advanced and economically successful nations.

We would then have a kind of two-tier world, with the top tier consisting of a global democratic civilization and an integrated world economy, and the bottom tier occupied by backward, failed, or otherwise marginalized nations. In many ways this would be an ugly world to live in, and the plight of the bottom tier would have ramifications that could not be wholly and neatly sealed off and kept beyond the confines of the democratic countries. There would be problems of access to raw materials, illegal immigration, refugee flows, famine, terrorism, drug trafficking, and a host of other difficulties to contend with—many of which we are already facing. The problems would become even more acute if major economic or political breakdowns were to afflict such strategically located countries as Algeria or Mexico. Yet none of this by itself would pose a mortal threat to democratic hegemony.

Democracy's preeminence can be seriously challenged only by an ideology with universalist aspirations that proves capable of coming to power in an economically advanced or militarily powerful nation. Though there are no convincing signs of the emergence of such an ideology at this time, it is worth taking a brief look at the major alternatives often cited as competitors to democracy.

The first of these is nationalism, which is clearly enjoying a resurgence in many parts of the world, even as its influence appears to be waning elsewhere. Nationalism, however, is not a universalist ideology, but a category that embraces a myriad of particularisms. Serbian nationalism and Croatian nationalism may share many formal similarities, but the former will have no appeal to Croats and the latter no appeal to Serbs. Moreover, nationalism as such does not mandate any particular kind of political order. One can find Russian nationalists, for example, who are communists, fascists, monarchists—or democrats. Nationalist passions may indeed threaten democracy in many specific circumstances, and ethnic strife can be a serious problem for established as well as new democracies. But in principle nationalism is by no means incompatible with democracy. In fact, as the case of the Baltic peoples makes clear, nationalist movements are often strongly democratic.

Turning next to religious doctrines, it is clear that radical or fundamentalist Islam is by far the most formidable competitor to democracy. Indeed, it is probably the most vital alternative to democracy to be found anywhere today. Only among Islamic peoples does opposition to dictatorial regimes frequently express itself in nondemocratic forms; in fact, in some Islamic countries free elections might well bring Islamist rather than democratic oppositions to power. Yet it is doubtful that fundamentalist Islam can pose a serious global challenge to democracy.

Although Islam holds the allegiance of more than eight hundred million people who dominate a wide area stretching from West Africa to Southeast Asia, it does not appear to be attracting many adherents outside the Islamic world. Moreover, it is highly questionable whether Islamic fundamentalism can become the basis for economically or militarily successful regimes. When it burst upon the scene a little over a decade ago, the Ayatollah Khomeini's Iran seemed to have tremendous revolutionary élan. Yet it proved incapable of winning a bitter war against a much smaller neighbor, of exporting the revolution to other Islamic countries, or of running a modern economy. It now appears to be following more moderate policies that may help to improve the economy and to stabilize the regime, but it no longer seems to represent even the Islamic wave of the future.

COUNTRIES TO WATCH

Another possible competitor to democracy would be a reinvigorated communism, but the events of August 1991 in the Soviet Union show how unlikely it is that the remaining communist regimes can regain their former vitality. Particularly telling was the fact that the coup plotters made no reference at all to communism in justifying their actions. Even in China, whose octogenarian rulers remain committed communists, knowledgeable observers say that hardly anyone under the age of forty still believes in Marxism-Leninism. Especially for an ideology oriented toward the future, the failure to attract the young is an unmistakable sign of decay. Communism today appears to be doomed to the fate that Moynihan foresaw for democracy in 1975: it is "a holdover form of government . . . which has simply no relevance to the future. It is where the world was, not where it is going."

The nature and the fate of the successor regimes in the Soviet Union and China will be of decisive importance for the future of democracy—not just because of their size and power but also because of the influence they can exert over Eastern Europe and East Asia respectively. If both these countries were successfully to follow the democratic path, the world might indeed approach Fukuyama's vision of an enduringly triumphant liberal democracy. But if they do not, they offer the most likely seedbeds for the birth of a new antidemocratic ideology.

Democrats have just gained the ascendancy in the Soviet Union, and the passing of Deng Xiaoping may open the way for a revival of the Chinese democratic movement that was so harshly repressed in Tiananmen Square. Yet there are also other important political currents and forces in both countries, including powerful military establishments. The emergence of a military-backed neoauthoritarian regime, possibly after a period of chaos or even civil war, may be as likely an outcome as a stable democracy in both Russia and China. Though a regime of this type might initially claim to be a temporary stop on the road toward democracy, it could easily wind up evolving in unpredictable and antidemocratic directions. And if such a regime were economically or militarily successful, it could quickly become an attractive model for other countries in its region and in the world.

Another possible source for a future alternative to liberal democracy may be Japan and the other noncommunist countries of East Asia. These countries have achieved spectacular economic progress through a synthesis of elements drawn from Confucian and other traditional influences, market economics, and democratic politics. The stability of democracy in Japan and the recent democratic openings in Korea and Taiwan could be taken as evidence of the triumph of liberal democracy in the region. Yet the political systems of these countries operate rather differently from those in the West. As Samuel P. Huntington has pointed out, "the East Asian dominant-party systems seem to involve competition for power but not alternation in power, and participation in elections for all, but participation in office only for those in the 'mainstream' party."[10]

It is not a foregone conclusion that the future will bring East Asia toward a greater convergence with Western-style liberal democracy; it might instead lead to an increased emphasis on those features that distinguish East Asian societies from the West. In that case, East Asia might gradually evolve a new ideology, which, given the extraordinary economic and technological dynamism of the region, could become extremely attractive to other nations as well.

Let us return, then, to the question with which we began: How long will the democratic moment last? I venture to predict that it will endure at least for the remainder of this century. Some recently established democracies will almost certainly fail during the coming decade, but other countries that are now under authoritarian or communist rule are likely to move toward democracy. Though it would be hazardous to forecast beyond that, the three key countries to watch in assessing the longer-term prospects for democracy in the world are Russia, China, and Japan.

There is one other key country, however, that has not yet been mentioned—the United States. If in 1980 a political analyst had sought to predict the future of communism on the basis of a survey of the international scene, he almost certainly would have gotten things very wrong; for he would have missed the most important factor—the largely hidden internal decay of the Soviet Union. This is certainly not meant to imply that the United States today is in an analogous situation. Yet as observers on all points of the U.S. political spectrum seem to agree, there are many reasons to worry about the political, economic, and cultural health of American democracy. A serious social or economic crisis in the United States would not only be terrible for Americans, it would have a devastating effect on the fortunes of democracy worldwide. Thus the highest priority for Americans must be to repair the fabric of our own democratic order.

That is not to advocate, however, that America "come home" and turn its back on its international responsibilities as the world's leading democracy. It is true that the energies and resources of the United States are not unlimited, but if properly directed, they are sufficient for both its domestic and international needs. There is no real conflict between improving democracy at home and supporting its spread and consolidation abroad. Just as the model provided by a healthy United States enhances the aspiration for democracy elsewhere, so the progress of the struggle for democracy around the world can give Americans renewed appreciation of the principles on which our country was founded and on which its future success depends.

II

THE TWIN PILLARS OF LIBERAL DEMOCRACY

3

The Role of Human Rights

1995

Human rights are the claims that all human beings are justly entitled to make merely by virtue of their being human. When this concept was introduced in the seventeenth century, these claims were described as *natural rights* and were said to be derived from the essential nature of every human individual. Over the centuries the more common term became first the *rights of man* and then *human rights*. This change reflected in part a broadening of the range of such rights to include claims that cannot easily be regarded as natural and that in some cases can be fulfilled only in a prosperous society.

The concept of human rights is intimately bound up with the development of modern democracy. *Democracy*, as the term is most often used today, comprises two essential elements: rule by the majority and the protection of individual human rights. Political rule by the majority of the citizens flourished in classical Greece; the notion of human rights, however, is a modern innovation. All previous moral and political teachings emphasized duties or obligations rather than rights. To the extent that rights were acknowledged at all, they were regarded as dependent on the political order to which one belonged, not as natural or universal rights.

Although some would trace the origin of the concept of human rights back to the Dutch jurist Hugo Grotius or even to earlier thinkers, the first fully elaborated doctrine of natural rights appeared in the work of Thomas Hobbes.[1] The key to Hobbes's political philosophy is his doctrine of the *state of nature*, the term he uses to describe the prepolitical situation that he regards as the natural human condition. According to Hobbes, all human beings are by nature equal, and each is dominated by the desire for self-preservation. As a result, where they are not governed by a sovereign power,

37

they are in a perpetual state of war with one another. In this situation, there is no law, and no actions can be considered unjust. Although human beings thus have no natural duties, they do possess the "right of nature": All individuals are free to do whatever they deem necessary for their own self-preservation.

Despite—indeed, because of—this unbounded liberty, human life in the state of nature is, in Hobbes's most famous phrase, "solitary, poor, nasty, brutish, and short." But reason suggests to human beings a way in which they may escape from the misery of their natural condition: They can mutually agree to transfer their natural right to all things to a sovereign power that will seek to preserve peace among them and defend them against external enemies. Thus the basis of all political orders is this covenant, or social contract, entered into voluntarily (though largely out of fear) by free and equal individuals in order to improve their own security.

Hobbes himself favored monarchy over republicanism and was a notorious champion of absolutism. Believing that the horrors occasioned by civil war were the greatest calamity that could befall human beings, he maintained that the rights of the sovereign should be unchecked and indivisible and that subjects have no right to withdraw their consent to obey the sovereign once it is given. (Even Hobbes, however, held that certain rights, such as that of resisting assaults upon one's life, are inalienable and cannot be transferred or renounced; in the same spirit, he opposed self-incrimination and the admissibility of evidence obtained through torture.) Yet the principles that he put forth were to become the basic framework of the liberal tradition: that human beings are naturally free, equal, and independent and that only their own consent can provide a sound and legitimate foundation for political rule. Unlike previous political thinkers, Hobbes taught that by nature the solitary individual and individual rights precede the political or social community and the duties owed to it.

One of those who adapted the Hobbesian framework to produce a teaching more favorable to the rights of subjects was Benedict de Spinoza, who proclaimed democracy to be the most natural form of government and the one most compatible with individual liberty.[2] The most influential exponent of a more liberal version of the doctrine of natural rights, however, was John Locke.[3]

Locke's teaching differs from that of Hobbes in some important ways. Although Locke follows Hobbes in characterizing humans in the state of nature as being perfectly free and equal and preeminently concerned with their own self-preservation, he also presents the state of nature as differing from the state of war. Locke claims that the state of nature is governed by a "law of nature" that teaches people not to harm one another. Yet he also asserts that in the state of nature individuals have the right to punish transgressions against the law of nature, including the right to destroy those who threaten them with destruction. Thus, however one finally interprets Locke's puzzling account of the law of nature, it is not surprising that he concludes that the rights of the individual in the state of nature are precarious and subject to repeated violation by others. And, like Hobbes, he prescribes as the remedy for the constant fears and dangers of the state of nature a voluntary agreement among individuals to form a political society.

According to Locke's account, however, individuals do not unreservedly transfer their natural rights to the sovereign when they establish a commonwealth. Because their very purpose in entering into political society is to secure the rights that they enjoy in the state of nature, it would be foolish and counterproductive for them to endow the sovereign with absolute, arbitrary power. Legitimate political power must be strictly confined to the pursuit of the public good of the society, which is understood as the preservation of the lives and possessions of those who compose it. Moreover, such power should be divided between a supreme legislative authority (preferably entrusted to an assembly whose members will themselves be subject to the laws they have made) and a subordinate executive. Even the legislative power, should it betray its trust, may be removed or altered by the people. Although Locke's teaching is not incompatible with limited monarchy, he clearly advocates the sovereignty of the people.

Locke formulated what became the classic trinity of natural rights—life, liberty, and property. For Hobbes, property did not exist in the state of nature. Locke, by contrast, tries to show that human labor can give a right to property outside the bounds of political society. Indeed, Locke sometimes seems to give property pride of place among the natural rights, asserting that the preservation of property is the goal of political society and stressing that government does not have the right to confiscate or even to tax the property of the people without their consent. Labor, Locke suggests, is essential not just for the bare preservation of human beings but for their comfort and security; hence they must be guaranteed secure property rights that will enable them to enjoy the fruits of their labor.

THE AMERICAN AND FRENCH REVOLUTIONS

The doctrine of natural rights, chiefly in its Lockean formulation, was to become the theoretical inspiration of both the American and French Revolutions, as reflected in the most famous documents of those revolutions. The American Declaration of Independence states: "We hold these truths to be self-evident, that all men are created equal, that they are endowed by their Creator with certain unalienable Rights, that among these are Life, Liberty and the pursuit of Happiness. That to secure these rights, Governments are instituted among Men, deriving their just powers from the consent of the governed. That whenever any Form of Government becomes destructive of these ends, it is the Right of the People to alter or to abolish it." And the Declaration of the Rights of Man and of the Citizen, issued by France's National Assembly in 1789, asserts: "The end of all political associations is the preservation of the natural and imprescriptible rights of man; and these rights are liberty, property, security, and resistance of oppression."

The French declaration also enumerates a variety of civil or political rights that citizens can expect their government to uphold as a way of fulfilling their basic natural rights. Similar guarantees of civil and political rights can be found in the U.S. Constitution and in the Bill of Rights, with which it was amended. These include the rule of law; various protections regarding the administration of criminal justice; freedom of religion, of speech, and of the press; protection of property rights; the institution of a separation of powers within the government; and the right of citizens to participate in choosing their representatives in the legislature.

Although theorists belonging to the Lockean tradition of natural rights strongly favor representative government, and thus a certain measure of majority rule, they often are highly critical of "democracy," particularly as it was practiced in the ancient republics. This viewpoint is evident in *Federalist* 10, in which James Madison asserts that the great flaw of popular government is its tendency toward oppression by a majority faction. Thus Madison argues that "pure," or direct, democracies, like those of antiquity, have always been incompatible with personal security and the rights of property. The goal of the new science of politics elaborated in *The Federalist*, whose chief principles are constitutionalism, representative government, and the separation of powers, is to combine popular sovereignty with the protection of every citizen's rights to life, liberty, and property.[4] The success of this project has been so great that today the defense of individual rights is generally regarded as a constitutive element of democracy.

THE INFLUENCE OF KANT

The doctrine of natural rights—grounded in rights that belong equally to all human beings—clearly is universalist in character. At the same time, however, this doctrine holds that political orders derive their being and their legitimacy only from the consent of those who are party to the social contract. The social contract embraces not the whole of humanity but only the members of a particular society, whose government is obliged to protect the life, liberty, and property of its own citizens. Moreover, the various political societies remain in a "state of nature" with one another, subject to no binding law or common power. Thus the citizens of one political order would appear to have no compelling interest in influencing how another sovereign power treats its own citizens or in securing the protection of human rights internationally.

The turn toward internationalizing the concept of human rights is associated with the thought of Immanuel Kant, who in his "Perpetual Peace" elaborates the idea of a federation of nations composed of states that have republican (that is, representative) governments.[5] According to Kant, republican government is the only kind appropriate to the rights of man, and it is also the most conducive to peace among nations. By establishing international concord, Kant's proposed federation would render more secure the rights to life, liberty, and property of individual citizens by protecting them against the danger of war, thus completing humanity's escape from the state of nature to a state of peace.

Kant also effects a far-reaching transformation in the qualitative understanding of human rights. In Kant's thought, human freedom is no longer understood primarily as a means for achieving the ends of self-preservation or the pursuit of happiness. Building upon the distinction, introduced by Jean-Jacques Rousseau, between natural liberty (which consists in following one's own inclinations) and civil, or moral, liberty (which consists in self-imposed obedience to law),[6] Kant identifies freedom with self-legislation. But he extends Rousseau's notion of the general will, which constitutes the self-legislation of a particular political community, into a principle of universal human morality.

The central principle of that morality—the "categorical imperative"—commands that human beings act only in accordance with maxims that they can also will to be universal laws.[7] Kant also offers a second formulation of the categorical imperative, which commands that we treat human beings always as ends and never only as means. By this standard, to violate the rights of others is to treat them as mere means and hence is morally impermissible. The rights of individuals must be respected not because they are naturally impelled to seek their self-preservation but because they are rational beings capable of obeying the moral law. According to Kant, it is because human beings are capable of morality that they alone have dignity.

The influence of Kant is immediately apparent when one turns to the most prominent human rights document of the twentieth century, the Universal Declaration of Human Rights proclaimed by the United Nations in 1948. Its preamble begins: "Whereas recognition of the inherent dignity and of the equal and inalienable rights of all members of the human family is the foundation of freedom, justice, and peace in the world." The first sentence of Article 1 ("All human beings are born free and equal in dignity and rights") also adds the Kantian emphasis on human dignity to the older language of inalienable rights.

ECONOMIC AND SOCIAL RIGHTS

The first twenty-one of the thirty articles of the Universal Declaration generally speak of the kinds of rights that are familiar from the eighteenth-century French Declaration of the Rights of Man and of the Citizen. Article 22, however, begins the enumeration of a new kind of rights: "Everyone, as a member of society, has the right to social security and is entitled to realization, through national effort and international cooperation and in accordance with the organization and resources of each State, of the economic, social and cultural rights indispensable for his dignity and the free development of his personality." The succeeding articles not only affirm the right to work and to join trade unions but also promote such entitlements as the right to leisure, including paid holidays; the right to an "adequate" standard of living and to financial security in the event of unemployment, sickness, and old age; the right to free compulsory elementary education; and the right to enjoy the arts. This section concludes with Article 28, which states that all are entitled to "a social and international order" in which the rights outlined in the Declaration can be fulfilled.

The inclusion of this new class of rights seems to reflect a kind of universalization of the goals of welfare-state liberalism, as embodied in Franklin D. Roosevelt's New Deal in the United States. Indeed, the preamble to the Universal Declaration explicitly cites the aspiration toward a world in which all will enjoy Roosevelt's famous "four freedoms"; these include not just freedom of speech and of belief but also freedom from fear and from want. Most governments, however, are not as capable of ensuring their citizens freedom from want as they are of guaranteeing freedom of speech or belief. The degree to which a government can honor these social and economic rights must depend on its own "resources" or on "international cooperation."

The question of whether such economic and social aspirations can properly be considered human rights remains a subject of both political and intellectual controversy. The United Nations has given equal status to economic, social, and cultural rights, on the one hand, and to political and civil rights, on the other. Twin International Covenants on these two classes of rights were adopted in 1966. Subsequent UN documents affirm not only that human rights are "indivisible" but that attainment of civil and political rights requires the enjoyment of economic and social rights and hence demands "effective" national and international development policies. More recent UN declarations have proclaimed a universal "right to development."

The cause of economic and social rights has been championed at the United Nations by representatives of developing countries and of communist countries. Critics of the UN doctrine on economic and social rights, however, charge that it allows authoritarian governments in poor countries to justify their failure to comply with political and civil rights by claiming that such noncompliance is the fault of richer countries that have inadequately provided them with international development assistance. The eminent Soviet dissident Andrei Sakharov argued that, contrary to the official state propaganda of communist countries emphasizing economic and social rights, it is really civil and political rights that guarantee individual liberty and give life to social and economic rights.[8]

In any case, it seems clear that the concept of economic and social rights reflected in UN documents represents a departure from the orientation that informed the natural rights tradition. The very notion of equal and inalienable rights traditionally extended only to those goods that individuals were naturally entitled (one might even say compelled) to seek, prior to and apart from their membership in any political society. In forming or joining themselves to a social contract, individuals transferred some portion of their natural rights to the community. In return, they became better able to achieve the ends they sought in the state of nature because of the security granted by the new rights they obtained as citizens. These civil and political rights offered them a protected sphere in which each could engage in the pursuit of happiness. The role of government was not to provide individuals with goods but to enable them to pursue their own goods.

This older tradition was by no means silent about economic rights. Indeed, it gave a central role to the right of property, founded on the natural right of individuals to enjoy the fruits of their own labor. It thus emphasized economic freedom (appropriately regulated by the political community) as opposed to economic entitlements. The UN Universal Declaration still includes the right of individuals to own property and not to be deprived of it arbitrarily (Article 17), but there is no longer any mention of property rights in the two International Covenants or in most subsequent UN declarations. Nonetheless, in the 1990s, with the fall of Soviet communism and the worldwide trend toward privatization, signs have appeared that the notion of a human right to property is coming back into favor. In fact, the draft Russian constitution proposed by President Boris Yeltsin in April 1993 proclaimed the inviolability of private property and even called it a natural right.

HUMAN RIGHTS AND INTERNATIONAL POLITICS

The issue of human rights moved to the forefront of international politics in the 1970s. During that decade the activities of the dissident human rights movement in the Soviet Union and Eastern Europe captured the attention and the imagination of the world. In the 1975 Helsinki Agreement of the Conference on Security and Cooperation in Europe (CSCE), the Soviet

Union and its allies, in exchange for gains they sought regarding economic and security issues, agreed to a series of Western-inspired human rights provisions. This public commitment on the part of their governments further energized the dissidents, and unofficial Helsinki Watch committees sprang up in both East and West to monitor compliance. Periodic CSCE review meetings provided a regular opportunity to call the communist countries to account and to bring worldwide attention to the plight of the dissidents. Many observers believe that the human rights movement made a crucial contribution to the subsequent collapse of European communism.

Human rights were brought to new prominence in U.S. foreign policy during the administration of Jimmy Carter, who made the promotion of international human rights a central focus of his presidency. A Bureau of Human Rights and Humanitarian Affairs was established in the State Department, and it was charged with compiling an annual report to Congress on the human rights performance of countries throughout the world. The brutal violations of human rights (including torture and "disappearances") in a number of Latin American countries during this period brought enhanced world attention to the issue. Several nongovernmental organizations dedicated to the worldwide struggle for human rights also rose to prominence, most notably Amnesty International, which was awarded the Nobel Peace Prize in 1977.

As the promotion of human rights was a central theme of U.S. foreign policy during the 1970s, so the promotion of democracy became a central theme during the 1980s. In part, this focus on democracy emerged because many dictatorial regimes, including some of the most flagrant abusers of human rights, weakened or fell, making transition to democracy seem a more feasible goal than it had seemed before. It also reflected, however, the view of Ronald Reagan's and George H. W. Bush's administrations that the negative side of human rights policy embodied in opposition to human rights abuses should be accompanied by a positive, long-term effort to foster democracy as the best safeguard of human rights. Bill Clinton's administration, which designated support for democracy as one of the three pillars of its foreign policy, appeared to aim at a synthesis of the Carter and Reagan-Bush approaches, and in 1994 it reorganized the Bureau of Human Rights and Humanitarian Affairs and renamed it the Bureau of Democracy, Human Rights, and Labor. Nonetheless, some political controversy, perhaps partly fueled by old partisan divisions, persisted regarding the relationship between human rights and democracy.

How one understands the relationship between human rights and democracy depends largely upon how one defines democracy. As noted at the outset of this chapter, today the term is generally reserved for regimes that are characterized by both majority rule and the protection of human rights—that is, for what often are called liberal or constitutional democracies. The relationship between democracy thus understood and human rights cannot by definition be anything but harmonious, in that failings in the protection of human rights would reduce a regime's claims to democracy. Another argument for the congruence between human rights and democracy lies in the fact that the Universal Declaration recognizes as a human right the right to take part in the government of one's country through voting in "periodic and genuine elections." Not only does democracy require the observance of human rights, but the observance of human rights requires democracy.

At the same time, it cannot be denied that an inevitable tension exists between what we have identified as the two essential aspects of democracy— rule by representatives of the majority and protection of the rights of individuals. As James Madison pointed out, majority rule in itself is no guarantee against oppression of the rights of unpopular minorities or individuals. There is no shortage of examples of democratically elected governments that, once in power, have trampled upon human rights. The tension between majority rule and human rights is acutely visible in Islamic countries with strong fundamentalist movements. To honor the results of free and fair elections in such countries, many observers claim, would be to bring to power governments that would harshly restrict human rights.

Just as it is possible for democratically elected rulers to violate human rights, in principle it would be possible for monarchs or other unelected rulers to honor individual rights. Yet autocrats would have to be extraordinarily benevolent indeed to tolerate expressions of freedom of speech, press, and assembly explicitly directed against their own right to rule. More generally, rulers who are not regularly accountable to an electorate and who do not expect to be bound by the laws they make have little personal incentive to protect individual rights. Although not all democratically elected governments scrupulously respect human rights, a glance at the contemporary world reveals that the only regimes that scrupulously respect human rights are democracies.

Nondemocratic governments vary greatly in the extent to which they violate human rights, and sometimes they may even marginally improve their conduct in response to external pressure. Democratic governments and nongovernmental organizations have had some success in inducing autocratic regimes to release individual political prisoners. Yet in no case has this kind of pressure ever produced a thoroughgoing change in a government's general stance toward human rights.

Human rights activists living within a nondemocratic regime may well couch their efforts, for reasons of prudence, in terms of getting their existing government to comply with its own laws or otherwise improve its own human rights performance. Yet those who take human rights seriously are almost invariably led to favor a democratic regime for their country as soon as circumstances permit. This position has certainly been adopted by such renowned human rights activists as Sakharov, Burmese democratic leader Aung San Suu Kyi, and exiled Chinese dissident Fang Lizhi. They have recognized that democracy—a regime based on majority rule through free elections, tempered by the separation of powers, the rule of law, and constitutional protections for individual liberties—provides countries with the only secure institutional framework for guaranteeing human rights in the contemporary world.

4

The Links between Liberalism and Democracy

1998

Less than a quarter century ago, democracy appeared to be confined, with a few exceptions, to North America and Western Europe. These nations had advanced industrial economies, sizable middle classes, and high literacy rates—factors that many political scientists regarded as prerequisites for successful democracy. They were home not only to free and competitive multiparty elections but also to the rule of law and the protection of individual liberties. In short, they were what had come to be called "liberal democracies."

In the rest of the world, by contrast, most countries were neither liberal nor democratic. They were ruled by a variety of dictatorships—military, single-party, revolutionary, Marxist-Leninist—that rejected free, multiparty elections (in practice, if not always in principle). By the early 1990s, however, this situation had changed dramatically, as an astonishing number of autocratic regimes around the world fell from power. They were generally succeeded by regimes that at least aspired to be democratic, giving rise to the phenomenon that Samuel P. Huntington termed the "third wave" of democratization.[1] Today, well over a hundred countries, in every continent in the world, can plausibly claim to have freely elected governments.

Outside of Africa, few of these aspiring new democracies have suffered outright reversions to authoritarianism. But many, even among those that hold unambiguously free and fair elections, fall short of providing the protection of individual liberties and adherence to the rule of law commonly found in the long-established democracies. As Larry Diamond has put it, many of the new regimes are "electoral democracies" but not "liberal democracies."[2] Citing Diamond's distinction, Huntington has argued that the introduction of elections in non-Western societies may often lead to victory by antiliberal forces.[3] And Fareed Zakaria has contended that the promotion of elections around the world has been responsible for "the rise of illiberal democracy"—that is, of freely elected governments that fail to safeguard basic liberties. "Constitutional liberalism," Zakaria argues, "is theoretically different and historically distinct from democracy. . . . Today the two strands of liberal democracy, interwoven in the Western political fabric, are coming apart in the rest of the world. Democracy is flourishing; constitutional liberalism is not." Drawing upon this distinction, Zakaria recommends that Western policymakers not only increase their efforts to foster constitutional liberalism but diminish their support for elections, and suggests that "liberal autocracies" are preferable to illiberal democracies.[4]

The basic distinction made by all these authors is both valid and important. Liberal democracy—which is what most people mean today when they speak of democracy—is indeed an interweaving of two different elements, one democratic in a stricter sense and the other liberal. As its etymological derivation suggests, the most basic meaning of the word "democracy" is the rule of the people. As the rule of the many, it is distinguished from monarchy (the rule of one person), aristocracy (the rule of the best), and oligarchy (the rule of the few). In the modern world, where the sheer size of states has rendered impossible the direct democracy once practiced by some ancient republics, the election of legislative representatives and other public officials is the chief mechanism by which the people exercise their rule. Today it is further presumed that democracy implies virtually universal adult suffrage and eligibility to run for office. Elections, then, are regarded as embodying the popular or majoritarian aspect of contemporary liberal democracy.

The word "liberal" in the phrase liberal democracy refers not to the matter of who rules but to the matter of how that rule is exercised. Above all, it implies that government is limited in its powers and its modes of acting. It is limited first by the rule of law, and especially by a fundamental law or constitution, but ultimately it is limited by the rights of the individual. The idea of natural or inalienable rights, which today are most commonly called "human rights," originated with liberalism. The primacy of individual rights means that the protection of the private sphere, along with the plurality and diversity of ends that people seek in their pursuit of happiness, is a key element of a liberal political order.

The fact that democracy and liberalism are not inseparably linked is proven by the historical existence both of nonliberal democracies and of liberal nondemocracies. The democracies of the ancient world, although their citizens were incomparably more involved in governing themselves than we are today, did not provide freedom of speech or religion, protection of private property, or constitutional government. On the other side, the birthplace of liberalism, modern England, retained a highly restricted franchise well into the nineteenth century. As Zakaria points out, England offers the classic example of democratization by a gradual extension of suffrage well after the essential institutions of constitutional liberalism were already in place. In our own time, Zakaria offers Hong Kong under British colonial rule as an example of a flourishing of liberalism in the absence of democracy.

ALL MEN ARE CREATED EQUAL

Although "unpacking" the component elements of modern liberal democracy is a crucial first step toward comprehending its character, overstating the disjunction between liberalism and democracy can easily lead to new misunderstanding. While many new electoral democracies fall short of liberalism, on the whole, countries that hold free elections are overwhelmingly more liberal than those that do not, and countries that protect civil liberties are overwhelmingly more likely to hold free elections than those that do not. This is not simply an accident. It is the result of powerful intrinsic links between electoral democracy and a liberal order.

Some of these links are immediately apparent. Starting from the democratic side, elections would seem to require the guarantee of certain civil liberties—the freedoms of speech, association, and assembly—if they are to be genuinely free and fair. Thus even minimalist definitions of democracy offered by political scientists usually include a stipulation that such liberties must be maintained at least to the extent necessary to make possible open electoral competition. If we begin instead with the human rights mandated by the liberal tradition, these are generally held today to include some kind of right to electoral participation. Thus Article 21 of the UN Universal Declaration of Human Rights states: "Everyone has the right to take part in the government of his country, directly or through freely chosen representatives. . . . The will of the people shall be the basis of the authority of the government; this will shall be expressed in periodic and genuine elections which shall be by universal and equal suffrage and shall be held by secret vote or by equivalent free voting procedures." One may regard this as a formal or even merely definitional link between liberalism and electoral democracy, but it points to a more profound kinship.

For the political doctrine at the source of liberalism also contains a deeply egalitarian and majoritarian dimension. This is the doctrine that all legitimate political power is derived from the consent of individuals, who are by nature not only free but equal. In the opening pages of his *Second Treatise of Government*, John Locke states that men are naturally in "a state of perfect freedom," which is "a state also of equality, wherein all the power and jurisdiction is reciprocal, no one having more than another: there being nothing more evident, than that Creatures of the same species and rank promiscuously born to all the same advantages of Nature, and the use of the same faculties, should be equal one amongst another without Subordination or Subjection."[5] The essential point is that no man has a natural claim to rule over another, and its clear corollary is that the rule of man over man can be justified only on the basis of a mutual agreement or "compact."

Now it is true that neither Locke nor his immediate successors concluded from this that democracy was the only legitimate form of government. For while they held that the consent of all is essential to the original compact that forms a political community, they also contended that the political community is free to decide where it chooses to bestow legislative power—whether it is in a democracy, an oligarchy, a monarchy, or a mixed government, as was the case in England. Liberalism did not originally insist on democracy as a form of government, but it unequivocally insisted upon the ultimate sovereignty of the people. Thus Locke argues that if the legislature is dissolved or violates its trust, the power to institute a new one reverts to the majority of the people.

In order to grasp the distinctive character of liberal egalitarianism, it is necessary to appreciate how different modern liberal democracy is from the premodern (and truly illiberal) democracy of the ancient city. Reliance on elected representation in the legislature, the key political institution of modern liberal democracy, was understood by its proponents as a decisive departure from ancient democracy. The authors of *The Federalist* frequently contrast two very different kinds of "popular government." In *Federalist* 10 they write in favor of a "republic" ("a government in which the scheme of representation takes place"), which they argue need not be subject to the infirmities of "a pure democracy" ("a society consisting of a small number of citizens who assemble and administer the government in person"). In pure or direct democracies, they contend, "there is nothing to check the inducements to sacrifice the weaker party or an obnoxious individual," and therefore they "have ever been found incompatible with personal security or the rights of property."[6] Later, in *Federalist* 63, acknowledging that the principle of representation was not unknown to the ancients, Madison states: "The true distinction between [ancient democracies] and the American governments *lies in the total exclusion of the people in their collective capacity, from any share in the latter, and not in the total exclusion of the representatives of the people from the administration of the former*" (italics in the original).[7] In short, modern liberal democracy from the outset was inclined to minimize the direct political role of the people. In this sense, Zakaria is on solid ground in stressing the antimajoritarian aspects of liberalism.

In part, of course, the substitution of representative government for direct democracy was justified by the larger size of modern states, which made it impractical for the whole people to assemble. But this very fact had led thinkers like Montesquieu and Rousseau to conclude that democratic or republican government was possible only in a small state, and Rousseau to assert that "the moment that a people adopts representatives it is no longer free."[8] There was, however, another ground used to justify representative government. In Madison's words, it "would refine and enlarge the public views by passing them through the medium of a chosen body of citizens, whose wisdom may best discern the true interest of their country and whose patriotism and love of justice will be least likely to sacrifice it to temporary or partial considerations."[9] In other words, elected representatives are expected to be superior to the average citizen. In the ancient democracies, by contrast, most public officials were chosen by lot. In *The Politics*, Aristotle characterizes lot as the democratic mode of choosing officials, and election as the oligarchic mode.[10] Montesquieu reiterates this judgment, adding, "lot is a method of election that does not distress anyone; it leaves each citizen a reasonable hope of serving his fatherland."[11] Where elections are used instead, those chosen tend to be richer, better educated, and more talented than most of their fellow citizens. In this light, representative or electoral democracy, besides largely eliminating the people from direct participation in self-government, also seems to constitute an aristocratic deviation from political equality.

BY AND FOR THE PEOPLE

Yet there is another sense in which modern liberal, representative democracy is much more egalitarian than was ancient democracy. In the latter, the citizens entitled to participate in public affairs invariably represented a relatively small percentage of the overall population. Not only were large numbers of slaves and resident aliens excluded, but women had no role in political affairs. Preliberal democracy, the direct democracy of the ancient city, was not based on any concept of the fundamental natural equality of all human beings. It is true, of course, that modern representative government for a long time excluded the poor and all women from political participation, and in the United States even coexisted with slavery. But it is no less true that these kinds of exclusions were always in tension with the underlying principle of liberalism—namely, that all human beings are by nature free and equal. The historical development of this principle inevitably transformed liberalism into liberal democracy.

It is one thing to claim that the majority of people in a traditional and hierarchical society have somehow given their tacit consent to a political arrangement in which they are excluded from having any voice. Popular sentiment in seventeenth-century England, if there had been a way of measuring it, might well have approved of a monarchical political system. But as the principle that all men are created equal gained currency, and as the educational and economic situation of the common people continued to improve, it was only to be expected that some of them would begin to demand the vote. And once they began to do so, how could it any longer be claimed that they consented to a political order in which they had no say? Popular sovereignty without popular government may be coherent in theory and even sustainable in practice for a time. Over the long run, however, popular sovereignty can hardly fail to lead to popular government.

Thus it is not surprising that, throughout the Western world, liberal constitutional regimes became more and more democratic during the nineteenth and twentieth centuries. The share of legislative power wielded by monarchs or unelected bodies receded until it had virtually disappeared. At the same time, suffrage was gradually broadened. Property qualifications and exclusions on the basis of race or sex were eliminated, to the point where "universal and equal suffrage" was endorsed by the world community in 1948 as a human right.

The moral grounds for extending suffrage are succinctly stated by John Stuart Mill in his *Considerations on Representative Government*, published in 1861.[12] "It is a personal injustice," Mill argues, "to withhold from anyone, unless for the prevention of greater evils, the ordinary privilege of having his voice reckoned in the disposal of affairs in which he has the same interest as other people. . . . No arrangement of the suffrage, therefore, can be permanently satisfactory in which any person or class is peremptorily excluded, in which the electoral privilege is not open to all persons of full age who desire to obtain it." On these grounds Mill also argues for the extension of the franchise to women. Yet this does not prevent him from arguing against granting the vote to illiterates and to recipients of parish relief (i.e., welfare); he also proposes that multiple votes be allotted to the educated and professional classes. Today, such departures from universality and equality in the allocation of the franchise seem shockingly "elitist." No arguments for "the prevention of greater evils" are reckoned as sufficiently powerful to overbalance the injustice of denying any citizen an equal vote.

MAKING DEMOCRACY WORK

There is another respect in which Mill's *Representative Government* is repugnant to contemporary sensibilities—namely, its justification of colonialism. For Mill, representative government "is the ideal type of the most perfect polity," but it is not applicable under all social conditions.[13] In particular, it is ill suited to "barbarous" or "backward" peoples, who are likely to need some form of monarchical or (preferably) external rule to bring them toward the state of civilization in which they might become fit for representative government.

In part, Mill's argument in favor of colonialism is grounded in a dubious doctrine of historical progress (or of "modernization," as we would say today). Yet there is another basis for Mill's contention that representative government is not applicable under all conditions that is not easily dismissed. As he puts it, "representative, like any other government, must be unsuitable in any case in which it cannot permanently subsist." If people do not value representative government, if they are unwilling to defend it, if they are unable to do what it requires, then they will not be able to maintain it. Thus it would be vain to expect that it would serve them well.

The concern with making democracy able to maintain itself, with training and spurring the people to do what is needed to make democracy work, is certainly not outdated. It is at the heart of most programs of "democracy assistance" now being provided to new democracies by Western governments, international and regional organizations, and nongovernmental organizations alike. It is at the root of the central concern today of political scientists who study new democracies—the problem of consolidation, or how to bring a democratic regime to the point where its breakdown becomes extremely unlikely. And it explains the widespread attention to issues of citizenship and civil society today, not only in new democracies but in long-established ones as well. These concerns reflect the irreducible fact that making self-government work is not easy. A democratic government can be given to any people, but not every people can maintain it. But what is to be done in the case of a people that is not, at least for the time being, capable of making democracy work? Mill's answer to this question was colonial rule. What is ours? That is the question implicitly raised by Zakaria's article.

The difficulty in answering it points to an acute tension within the modern democratic tradition between the liberal doctrine of just or legitimate government and the practical requirements of popular government. (In *The Social Contract*, Rousseau says, "All legitimate government is republican." But later in the same work he says, "Freedom is not a fruit of every climate, and it is not therefore within the capacity of every people."[14]) The principle that all men are born free and equal, and that no one has a right to rule them without their consent, has now swept the world. As I have argued above, this has inevitably come to be understood as meaning that they cannot be ruled without their clearly expressed consent, in the form of an election. Yet the experience of past ages and of many lands suggests that this principle cannot be effectively put into practice everywhere and immediately. The failure in the 1960s of so many of the democracies bequeathed by the departing colonial powers once again demonstrated the fact that under certain conditions democracy is unlikely to endure. But if democratic government is required everywhere in principle, what course can a good liberal democrat follow where it appears unable to work in practice? This conundrum largely accounts for the alternating cycles of euphoria and despair about the prospects for the spread of liberal democracy.

How does Zakaria suggest that this dilemma be resolved? He contends, first, that constitutionalism, the rule of law, and the protection of individual liberty are more essential than representative government. Accordingly, he recommends that, rather than encouraging the introduction of elections in many developing countries, Western policy should favor the establishment of "liberal autocracy." As noted above, the prime example of liberal autocracy that he presents is nineteenth-century Europe, where the introduction of constitutional liberalism by monarchical governments preceded democratization. It has often been remarked that the sequence of first liberal constitutionalism, then gradual democratization, can have advantages in accustoming people to the requirements of self-government. But is this a practical strategy today?

During the nineteenth and early twentieth centuries, democratization proceeded in a context in which more traditional principles of social hierarchy still had a considerable hold over the popular imagination. The idea of equality had not been fully accepted as the preeminent principle of political legitimacy. Monarchy and aristocracy still prevailed in most of Europe, so that even a limited legislative role for an assembly elected with a restricted suffrage could seem like progress toward popular government. Today the situation is dramatically different. There are only a few countries—principally Islamic monarchies—in which anything like traditional rule still holds sway. In these cases, perhaps the nineteenth-century European model can to some extent be emulated. Elsewhere, existing autocracies—or the regimes that aspiring democracies have replaced—are generally ideological rather than traditional regimes and espouse some kind of egalitarian doctrine of their own. In a postcommunist or formerly one-party socialist regime, what principle could be accepted as a basis for restricting suffrage? And what legitimate mechanism other than election could be used for deciding who will rule?

The only example in the contemporary world of liberal autocracy that Zakaria explicitly cites is British-ruled Hong Kong. Yet he certainly does not seem prepared to recommend a revival of colonialism. Earlier in the 1990s, there was a flurry of discussion of the problem of "failed states"—former client states of the superpowers during the Cold War that threatened to collapse once the support of their patron had been withdrawn. Amid the talk of a new world order, there seemed to be some inclination to have the "international community" intervene in such cases, in effect reviving something like colonial rule under the aegis of the United Nations. Whatever the merits or the feasibility of this idea, the fiasco of the U.S. attempt at political (as opposed to humanitarian) intervention in Somalia, along with the proliferation of states that might have been candidates for such costly international reconstruction operations, quickly made it clear that the political will for this kind of policy was lacking.

The practical model that Zakaria seems to have in mind is the economically successful autocracies of East Asia. Yet it would surely be questionable to assert that these autocracies are genuinely constitutional or liberal, a fact that Zakaria himself seems to recognize by characterizing Indonesia, Singapore, and Malaysia not as "liberal" but only as "liberalizing" autocracies. It would be implausible indeed to claim that these states more reliably protect individual rights or have more independent and impartial judiciaries than the Latin American democracies that Zakaria describes as "illiberal." Even the Singaporeans themselves, while claiming to practice democracy, acknowledge that their regime, to quote Singapore's UN Ambassador, Bilahari Kausikan, "has never pretended or aspired to be liberal."[15] Thus, despite Zakaria's talk of constitutionalism and individual rights, he seems to wind up taking the much more familiar view that authoritarian capitalist development is the most reliable road to eventual liberal democracy.

The economic achievements of these East Asian autocracies have certainly been impressive, but so have been the economic achievements of East Asian democracies, beginning with Japan. This is not the place to enter into the complex and hotly contested argument about to what extent, if at all, authoritarian rule has been responsible for Asian economic development. What is clear, however, is that in the rest of the world the overall record of autocracies in promoting economic development, let alone the growth of constitutional liberalism, has been poor. As Mill noted, the same shortcomings that make a people poorly prepared for representative government are also likely to be found in its unelected rulers. Wise and benevolent despots are the exception, not the rule.

THE USES AND LIMITS OF ELECTIONS

It was only to be expected that, as countries around the world replaced their autocratic regimes with freely elected ones, they would encounter serious difficulties in making democracy work. Self-government is indeed difficult, and holding elections is merely one step in a long and arduous process that, in the best case, will culminate in a consolidated liberal democracy. Electorates can make bad choices as well as good or (most often) mediocre ones. Demagogues can use electoral campaigns to appeal to voters' worst instincts, including ethnic or religious intolerance (although the number of new democracies in which candidates have succeeded on the basis of such appeals is far fewer than might have been expected). But in any case, how often can elections themselves be plausibly cited as the cause of problems that would not have been just as likely to persist or arise under a nonelected government? African voters, for example, may often cast their ballots along ethnic or tribal lines, but in how many African countries have dictatorial governments achieved real ethnic accommodation, rather than merely the domination of some groups by others? Most new democracies are undoubtedly confronting severe challenges, but almost none of these would be overcome by abolishing elections.

It is also true that, beyond peacefully getting rid of a bad and unpopular government (which is no small accomplishment), elections by themselves do not solve most other political problems. For this and other reasons, prudence counsels against hastily pushing elections on a fairly stable, decent, and moderate nondemocratic regime, especially in a country where the strongest opposition forces are not themselves well disposed toward liberal democracy. This, however, is a lesson that most Western governments, inherently inclined toward diplomatic caution, hardly need to be taught. In fact, their adherence to such a policy is a frequent complaint of those who accuse Western governments of being too friendly with nondemocratic governments, especially in the Arab world.

There are arguably cases where elections have made things worse, as in Angola in 1992, where Jonas Savimbi's refusal to accept his defeat in a UN-supervised election led to a violent escalation of that country's civil war. Yet despite some serious setbacks, the overall record of attempts to use internationally supervised elections as a method of conflict resolution for countries embroiled in civil strife has been surprisingly positive. This relatively recent innovation, first attempted in Nicaragua in 1990, combines peacemaking with democracy building, but is driven primarily by the former goal. Thus elections are often held under extraordinarily difficult circumstances and at times that would not have been chosen if democracy building were the only goal. Nonetheless, such elections have not only brought a number of bloody civil wars to a halt, but in countries like Mozambique and El Salvador have had positive political results as well. Even if such countries today are merely illiberal democracies, they are manifestly much better off than if they were still racked by civil war. Afghanistan, a country that did not undergo an electoral process and faces continuing civil war and the rule of an extremist and intolerant Islamist government, does not present a very attractive alternative model.

In more typical cases of democratic transition, where an authoritarian government either is overthrown or negotiates an agreement with domestic opposition forces on the creation of a new regime, the timing of "founding elections" can be a matter of critical importance for the success of an emerging democracy. In such cases there is room for reasonable disagreement about how soon to hold elections. Amid the devastated political landscape of the post-Mobutu Congo, for example, even those committed to trying to move the country in a democratic direction are divided about both the practicability and the desirability of conducting early elections. At the same time, it is difficult to see how dispensing with elections would lead the government of Laurent Kabila to move toward "constitutional liberalism," or how such unaccountable rule would be preferable to "illiberal democracy."

IF AT FIRST YOU DON'T SUCCEED

In such unfavorable situations, of course, electoral democracies may simply be unable to endure. The history of democratization is replete with failed attempts. That is why the pattern discerned by Huntington is also characterized by "reverse waves," periods when democratic breakdowns far outnumber democratic transitions. But the overall trend, nonetheless, is for more and more countries to become and remain democratic. Moreover, the historical record shows that countries that have had an earlier experience with democracy that failed are more likely to succeed in a subsequent attempt than countries with no previous democratic experience. So even if democracy breaks down, it can leave a legacy of hope for the future.

Now that a growing number of countries lacking the standard social and economic "prerequisites" for democracy have gained the privilege of electing their own leaders, it is not surprising that these new regimes often have serious deficiencies with respect to accountability, the rule of law, and the protection of individual liberties. There is every reason for Western nations to do all they can to assist these countries in improving their electoral democracies and turning them into liberal democracies. It is precisely the illiberal democracies that Zakaria maligns that are likely to be the most receptive audience for the promotion of constitutional liberalism that he recommends. For the road to constitutional liberalism in today's world runs not through unaccountable autocracies but through freely elected governments.

5

Why Liberalism Became Democratic

1999

Today the most liberal regimes in the world, those of the advanced Western countries, are typically referred to either as liberal democracies or, more often, simply as democracies. This reflects one of the most striking ways in which twentieth-century liberalism differs from the older liberalism that emerged in the late seventeenth and eighteenth centuries. Today, wherever one finds liberalism (understood as constitutional and limited government, the rule of law, and the protection of individual rights), it is almost invariably coupled with democracy (understood as the selection of government officials by universal suffrage). The converse proposition, however, has in recent decades been becoming less and less true. With the downfall since 1975 of scores of authoritarian regimes and their replacement by more or less freely elected governments, there are now many regimes that can plausibly be called democratic but not liberal. As a result, the relationship between liberalism and democracy has once again become a subject of intense intellectual and policy debate.

Perhaps the most prominent example of this, as noted in previous chapters, is Fareed Zakaria's 1997 article in *Foreign Affairs* on "The Rise of Illiberal Democracy."[1] Zakaria emphasizes a point that had already been made by other observers more sympathetic than he to the struggles of new would-be liberal democracies in the postcommunist and developing worlds: Even among those regimes that have succeeded in holding genuinely free elections, many have compiled a poor record in terms of such criteria of liberalism as the rule of law and the protection of individual rights. The more sympathetic observers tend to stress the importance of "consolidating" these new democracies, preserving their electoral achievements while strengthening their liberal features. Zakaria, however, concludes that the liberal deficit of these regimes has emerged not in spite of, but in some measure because of, their adoption of the democratic mechanism of popular elections. He thus questions the wisdom of encouraging countries to elect their rulers before the foundations of liberalism are firmly in place.

Zakaria puts heavy emphasis on the distinction between liberalism and democracy. Making it clear that he views the former as more important than the latter, he argues for the superiority of liberal autocracy over illiberal democracy. This in turn has prompted discussion of whether liberal autocracy (or, more generically, nondemocratic liberalism) is still viable in the contemporary world. For the chief example of liberal autocracy that Zakaria provides is the constitutional monarchies of nineteenth-century Europe. They certainly did have many of the elements of liberalism in place before they adopted universal manhood suffrage. But it is also noteworthy that all of these pre-twentieth-century liberal nondemocracies have now become democratic. This raises the question of why liberal regimes have all tended to evolve in a democratic direction. Is it due merely to adventitious circumstances or extraneous factors, or is it somehow related to the intrinsic principles of liberalism? That is the issue I wish to explore.

LIBERALISM AND EQUALITY

Liberalism is essentially a doctrine devoted to protecting the rights of the individual to life, liberty, property, and the pursuit of happiness. Government is needed to protect those rights, but it can threaten them as well, so it is also essential to guard against their infringement by government. Thus liberalism entails a government that is limited by a constitution and by the rule of law. At first sight, however, there does not seem to be any reason in principle why such a government must be chosen by the people. A constitutional government of one man or of a few could rule in such a way as to protect the rights of individuals. Indeed, there is reason to fear that a government responsive to popular majorities will be tempted to violate the rights of unpopular individuals or minorities. Accordingly, many liberals in past centuries opposed the extension of the suffrage, fearing precisely such an outcome. Yet everywhere efforts to forestall the extension of the suffrage failed, and liberalism turned into liberal democracy. And far from being destroyed by its democratization, liberalism on the whole has flourished. This suggests that the tension between liberalism and democracy is not so great as some have thought. In fact, I would go further, and propose that the philosophy of liberalism contains within itself the seeds of its own democratization.

In the first place, one may point to the massive fact that the classic statements of liberal principles set forth not only the doctrines of individual rights and limited government but also the doctrine of human equality. The American Declaration of Independence proclaims as the first of its self-evident truths "that all men are created equal." The French Declaration of the Rights of Man and of the Citizen states in the very first of its seventeeen principles: "Men are born, and always continue, free and equal in respect of their rights." As was emphasized in the preceding chapters, this intimate connection between the rights or freedom of men and their mutual equality can easily be traced back to the classic work of liberal political theory, John Locke's *Second Treatise of Government*. In elaborating the origins of legitimate political power, Locke begins by considering "what state all men are naturally in"; he argues that this is not only "a state of perfect freedom" but "a state also of equality."[2]

The connection between natural liberty and natural equality is clear. If men are not equal in their natural rights—that is, if some men have a right to rule over other men—then men cannot naturally be free. And correspondingly, if all men are naturally free, then none can have a natural right to rule over others. Locke's *Second Treatise* is, of course, the sequel to his *First Treatise*, a refutation of Sir Robert Filmer's doctrine of paternal power. According to Locke, the ground of Filmer's system is as follows: "Men are not born free, and therefore could never have the liberty to choose either governors or forms of government."[3] After showing the flaws in Filmer's argument for the natural subjection of men, Locke begins the *Second Treatise* by asserting that if fraud and violence are not to be the only basis for government, a new origin for political power must be found. He finds it in the consent of the people. Precisely because men are "by nature all free, equal, and independent, no one can be put out of this estate and subjected to the political power of another without his own consent."[4] Once other principles of political legitimacy are undermined, only the consent of the governed remains.

To say that legitimate government rests on the consent of the governed is to say that the people—a term that for Locke means not the many as opposed to the nobles, but all those who belong to the society—are ultimately sovereign. They are the founders of political society; they decide where to invest the power of making laws; and they have "a right to resume their original liberty" and to choose a new legislative power if the existing one betrays their trust.[5] Yet despite these egalitarian or democratizing aspects of Locke's doctrine, he does not draw from it the conclusion that the people themselves (or their elected representatives) should necessarily govern. Instead, he argues that when men first unite into political society, the majority may choose to invest the legislative power not in themselves (which Locke says would constitute a "perfect democracy") but in a few men, or in a single man, or in such "compounded and mixed forms of government, as they think good."[6] In England, for example, he suggests that it is the attachment of the people to their old constitutional arrangements that keeps bringing them back to the "old legislative of king, lords, and commons."[7] In short, nondemocratic forms of government can be legitimate if they enjoy the consent of the people.

This is not unreasonable as theory, and it is a view that prevailed for at least a century among supporters of the rights of man and limited government. But gradually and inexorably the notion that government must be based on popular consent led to the notion that government must be of the people, by the people, and for the people. Why did this happen? Perhaps one may begin to address this question by asking why the people might consent to government that is *not* in the hands of themselves or their elected representatives. One may, of course, simply say that in earlier centuries the people were never really given a choice, and if they had been, they would have chosen popular government. Alternatively, one may conclude with Locke that "people are not so easily got out of their old forms as some are apt to suggest. They are hardly to be prevailed with to amend the acknowledged faults in the frame they have been accustomed to."[8] In the seventeenth and eighteenth centuries the monarchic and aristocratic principles still reigned not only in the world but in the minds of the people. One might say that the people were willing to consent to be ruled by others precisely because principles other than that of consent still held great sway. But the public espousal and growing acceptance of the principles of natural equality and government by consent were fated to erode the willingness of the people to consent to nondemocratic government.

In the American colonies, where Locke's teachings were most widely adopted and where monarchy and aristocracy enjoyed much less support than in the more traditional societies of Europe, it was clear after the Revolution that the people would accept nothing other than popular government.[9] The French Revolution quickly moved toward an outright rejection of any admixture of monarchy or aristocracy. Even in Britain, where popular attachment to the "old forms" remained much stronger, calls for universal manhood suffrage date back at least to the 1770s,[10] and the nineteenth century was marked by widespread and eventually successful agitation for expansion of the franchise.

EXTENDING THE VOTE

One useful way to explore the dynamic that led to the democratization of liberalism is to consider the views expressed by some leading liberal thinkers of the late eighteenth and the nineteenth century. An early example of the invocation of natural equality and consent of the people as a basis for rejecting anything other than popular government can be found in the work of Thomas Paine, who can always be counted upon to draw the most radical conclusions from the Lockean teaching on natural rights. In his *Dissertation on First Principles of Government*,[11] Paine argues that there are only two "primary divisions" of government: "First, government by election and representation; secondly, government by hereditary succession." The former, Paine contends, is "founded on the rights of the people," while the latter is "founded on usurpation." Hereditary government, according to Paine, "has not a right to exist." The English parliament may have had a right to call William and Mary to the throne in 1688, for "every Nation, for the time being, has a right to govern itself as it pleases." But Parliament had no right to bind future generations of Englishmen to be governed by the heirs of William and Mary.

As for representative government, its only true basis is equality of rights: "Every man has a right to one vote and no more in the choice of representatives." Though Paine does not address the question of female suffrage, he decries as unjust the view that property should be made the criterion for voting. Exclusion from voting is offensive because it "implies a stigma on the moral character of the persons excluded," and poverty does not justify such a stigma. "The right of voting for representatives," Paine holds, "is the primary right by which other rights are protected. To take away this right is to reduce a man to slavery, for slavery consists in being subject to the will of another, and he that has not a vote in the election of representatives is in this case."

Finally, I quote at some length a passage that, when allowances are made for Paine's excessive rhetoric, offers some insight into the historical process by which exclusion from voting came to seem intolerable:

> While men could be persuaded they had no rights, or that rights appertained only to a certain class of men, or that government was a thing existing in right of itself, it was not difficult to govern them authoritatively. The ignorance in which they were held and the superstition in which they were instructed furnished the means of doing it. But when the ignorance is gone and the superstition with it, when they perceive the imposition that has been acted upon them, when they reflect that the cultivator and the manufacturer are the primary means of all the wealth that exists in the world beyond what nature spontaneously produces, when they begin to feel their consequences by their usefulness and their right as members of society, it is then no longer possible to govern them as before. The fraud once detected cannot be reacted.

Another strand of support for extension of the suffrage came from utilitarianism, which, although it rejected the doctrine of natural rights, nonetheless took as a guiding principle Jeremy Bentham's dictum "Everyone to count for one, nobody for more than one." The classic expression of utilitarian political thought is considered to be James Mill's *Essay on Government*.[12] Like

Paine, James Mill regards the system of representation as the key to good government. Eschewing any language claiming the *right* of individuals to vote for their representatives, he argues that "the benefits of the representative system are lost in all cases in which the interests of the choosing body are not the same with those of the community." This coincidence of interests, however, may exist with less than universal suffrage, provided that the interests of those excluded from voting "are indisputably included in those of other individuals" who can vote. On this basis Mill justifies the exclusion of women, "the interest of almost all of whom is involved in that of their fathers or in that of their husbands," and is prepared to accept the exclusion of men under the age of forty, because "the men of forty have a deep interest in the welfare of the younger men."

James Mill also presents a long and convoluted argument on the question of property qualifications for voting. He rejects a high property qualification on the grounds that it would lead to a government of the few, who, given human nature, would pursue their own interests at the expense of the community's. Though he concedes that a very low qualification permitting the great majority of the people to vote would be "no evil," he also concludes that it would be "of no use," since admitting the small remainder to the suffrage would not change things much. Thomas Babington Macaulay, in his famous 1829 review of Mill's *Essay*, interprets Mill as being opposed to any property qualification and takes issue with him on this point.[13] (Macaulay also objects to Mill's reasoning on the question of women's suffrage, charging that the latter "placidly dogmatises away the interests of one half of the human race.")

For Macaulay, who also fundamentally objects to Mill's deductive approach to politics and his rapacious view of human nature, the issue of a "pecuniary qualification" for the vote is "the most important practical question in the whole essay." He argues, contrary to Mill, that since "it happens that in all civilised communities there is a small minority of rich men, and a great majority of poor men," it would indeed be in the interests of the latter, if they enjoyed the franchise, to use their political power to plunder the rich. In a marvelous rhetorical flight, Macaulay paints the dangers of enfranchising the poor:

[I]s it possible that in the bosom of civilisation itself may be engendered the malady which shall destroy it? Is it possible that institutions may be established which, without the help of earthquake, of famine, of pestilence, or of the foreign sword, may undo the work of so many ages of wisdom and glory, and gradually sweep away taste, literature, science, commerce, manufactures, everything but the rude arts necessary to the support of animal life? Is it possible that, in two or three hundred years, a few lean and half-naked fishermen may divide with owls and foxes the ruins of the greatest European cities, may wash their nets amidst the relics of her gigantic docks, and build their huts out of the capitals of her stately cathedrals? If the principles of Mr. Mill be sound, we say, without hesitation, that the form of government which he recommends will assuredly produce all this. But, if these principles be unsound, if the reasonings by which we have opposed them be just, the higher and middling orders are the natural representatives of the human race. Their interest may be opposed in some things to that of their poorer contemporaries; but it is identical with that of the innumerable generations which are to follow.

Macaulay's paeans to the splendors of civilization and his incomparable prose should not obscure the fact that this remains a dispute about "pecuniary qualification," which turns essentially on the likely fate of property under a regime of universal suffrage. This is a controversy that, one might say, is carried on within a wholly Lockean framework. The real issue is whether the right to property is endangered by the extension of the right to vote. As support for hereditary institutions faded with the triumph of the principles of natural equality and government by consent, the argument over democracy increasingly became an intraliberal dispute.

THE INEVITABILITY OF UNIVERSAL SUFFRAGE

In the debate over the potential consequences of eliminating property qualifications, the example of America often figured prominently. In his critique of James Mill's argument for universal manhood suffrage, Macaulay states, "The case of the United States is not in point," because there, unlike in more settled countries, the poor have a reasonable hope of becoming rich. Then, invoking the Malthusian doctrine that increased population will lead to greater inequality of conditions, he concludes, "As for America, we appeal to the twentieth century."

Tocqueville, of course, provided powerful ammunition in his *Democracy in America* for those who believed that universal suffrage would be compatible with the security of property. Among the many passages in which Tocqueville remarks upon the respect of the Americans for property, we may cite the following: "In no country in the world is the love of property more active and more anxious than in the United States; nowhere does the majority display less inclination for those principles which threaten to alter, in whatever manner, the laws of property."[14]

In addition to the more general argument he makes that the world has for seven hundred years been undergoing a providential and irresistible democratic revolution, Tocqueville also offers a more specific argument as to why continuing expansion of the suffrage is inevitable:

When a nation begins to modify the elective qualification, it may easily be foreseen that, sooner or later, that qualification will be entirely abolished.

There is no more invariable rule in the history of society: the further electoral rights are extended, the greater is the need for extending them; for after each concession the strength of the democracy increases, and its demands increase with its strength. The ambition of those who are below the appointed rate is irritated in exact proportion to the great number of those who are above it. The exception at last becomes the rule, concession follows concession, and no stop can be made short of universal suffrage.[15]

In describing the process by which the property qualifications existing prior to the American Revolution were gradually eliminated, Tocqueville notes that it was men of the higher orders who voted these changes, pursuing the goodwill of the people at any price. This in some ways seems to have characterized the process in Britain as well. Historian Gertrude Himmelfarb describes the struggle over the Reform Act of 1867 between Disraeli's Tories and Gladstone's Liberals in the following terms: "What is interesting is the fact that it was not the reformers inside or outside the House who forced up the price of reform, but rather the party leaders themselves. [Liberal parliamentarian Robert] Lowe described the parties as competing against each other in a miserable auction with the constitution being 'knocked down to the lowest bidder.' A Conservative complained that his colleagues were trying to 'outbid the Liberal party in the market of liberalism.'"[16]

In the wake of the passage of the Reform Act, even those most dubious about universal suffrage acknowledged its inevitability. In *Liberty, Equality, Fraternity*, James Fitzjames Stephen writes:

The accepted theory of government appears to be that everybody should have a vote, that the Legislature should be elected by these votes, and that it should conduct all the public business of the country through a committee which succeeds for the time in obtaining its confidence. This theory, beyond all question, has gone forth, and is going forth conquering and to conquer. The fact of its triumph is as clear as the sun at noonday, and the probability that its triumphs will continue for a longer time than we need care to think about is as strong as any such probability can well be. . . . If I am asked, What do you propose to substitute for universal suffrage? Practically, What have you to recommend? I answer at once, Nothing. The whole current of thought and feeling, the whole stream of human affairs, is setting with irresistible force in that direction. The old ways of living, many of which were just as bad in their time as any of our devices can be in ours, are breaking down all over Europe, and are floating this way and that like haycocks in a flood. Nor do I see why any wise man should expend much thought or trouble on trying to save their wrecks. The waters are out and no human force can turn them back, but I do not see why as we go with the stream we need sing Hallelujah to the river god.[17]

Stephen's somewhat half-hearted criticisms of democracy mostly focus on the importance of specialized knowledge and steadiness in the business of government and on the ignorance and fickleness of the voting masses.

He also echoes some of the concerns put forth by John Stuart Mill regarding the "mediocrity" of contemporary society and government.[18] And he attributes the enthusiasm for equality in part to "the enormous development of wealth in the United States." Like Macaulay, Stephen raises the question of how long the Americans "will continue to be equal when the population becomes dense," and concludes by wondering in any case whether "the rapid production of an immense multitude of commonplace, self-satisfied, and essentially slight people is an exploit which the whole world need fall down and worship."

Stephen's resigned and ineffectual grumblings largely reflect the subsequent course of opposition to universal suffrage, which turned from a political program into a cultural lament. With the first half of the twentieth century, the exclusion of women from the suffrage also began to be swept away. Thus when in 1948 the United Nations adopted the Universal Declaration of Human Rights, Article 21 stated, "The will of the people shall be the basis of the authority of the government; this will shall be expressed in periodic and genuine elections which shall be by universal and equal suffrage." Obviously, the provision of Article 21 calling for "genuine" elections has been consistently violated by many UN member states with one-party or other dictatorial governments, but even most of these (excepting, of course, South Africa under apartheid) have conducted their bogus elections under rules calling for universal and equal suffrage.

DEMOCRACY AND THE LIBERAL REVIVAL

What conclusions may be drawn from this brief survey of the evolution of liberalism into contemporary liberal democracy? First, the spread of liberal ideas of the natural freedom and equality of all human beings doomed any special and substantial privileges enjoyed on the basis of heredity. Though monarchy and even an aristocratic branch of the legislature may in some places have been preserved in form, everywhere in the developed world they have been emptied of any substantial political power. Second, these same liberal ideas eventually undermined any effort to exclude people from political participation on the basis of such factors as race, religion, or sex. Third, the attempt to limit the franchise on the basis of property qualifications was the greatest potential obstacle to the democratization of liberalism, because it could claim some basis in the sacredness of private property endorsed by liberalism itself.

The real or perceived tension between political majoritarianism and policies that promote economic growth and prosperity is a theme that remains very much alive today, with many commentators claiming that effective economic reform requires the insulation of policymakers from electoral majorities. At the same time, the history of the past two centuries has made it unmistakably clear that the introduction of universal suffrage need not lead to the outright plunder of the rich and the destruction of a productive economy and a civilized society. Tocqueville was right and Macaulay was wrong. The case of the nineteenth-century United States was indeed "in point." Its economic vitality and political stability were not simply the product of a sparse population able to expand over a vast and fertile continent. In the Old World as well, liberal societies have tended to generate large middle classes rather than to become divided into a handful of the rich and a vast majority of the poor.

At the same time, until the past two decades it could plausibly have been argued that, due to the social and economic policies enacted by popular majorities, liberalism was dying a slow death. With the spread of stated-owned industry, the seemingly irreversible growth of the welfare state, and the increasing tax burden necessary to pay for it, it was not unreasonable to view the political empowerment of the masses as proceeding in tandem with the gradual socialization of the economy. The idea of property rights seemed to be falling into increasing disrepute. One striking symptom of this was the omission from the UN International Covenant on Economic, Social, and Cultural Rights (1966) of any mention of the right to property (which had still featured in the 1948 Universal Declaration). Those political forces identifying themselves as liberals (in the European sense) were a dwindling minority, and ruling parties in many democracies identified themselves as socialists or social democrats. The term social (or even socialist) democracy often superseded the term liberal democracy. And of course, the democratic world was threatened by a powerful communist adversary that proclaimed both its egalitarianism and its hostility to liberalism.

The last two decades, however, have seen a remarkable revival of liberalism. Market economics has come back into vogue. State-owned industries are being privatized, and welfare benefits trimmed. The critical importance of protecting property rights has been recognized not only in international agreements and new national constitutions but by an influential academic literature. Right-of-center and explicitly promarket parties governed the leading democracies during the 1980s. Left-of-center parties, many of which have returned to power in the 1990s, have largely abandoned statist economics and rediscovered the virtues of markets and entrepreneurship. And all this has been accompanied and accelerated by the downfall of communism.

How have these developments and the liberal revival they have promoted affected the political role of popular majorities? Here I believe a crucial distinction must be made, one that is rooted in the very principles of liberalism. For I would say that the principle of universal inclusion—that no one should be deprived of an equal voice in choosing those who govern—has only become more sacrosanct. At the same time, however, there has been a clear weakening of the view that popular majorities should play a more active role in deciding on governmental policies.

The latter is reflected in many ways, but perhaps not least in the unfavorable connotation that the word "populism" has come to acquire in the new democracies of the developing and postcommunist worlds. More generally, there has been no tendency, in either new or long-established democracies, to make governments more directly responsive to the electorate through such traditional devices as shortening terms of office. In fact, there has been an increasing trend toward giving greater power to judiciaries and autonomous agencies, the parts of government most insulated from the people. Judicial review was long viewed as an "antidemocratic" institution, giving power to unelected judges at the expense of popular majorities. In recent years, however, judicial review, once a peculiarity of the United States, has spread to old and new democracies alike. Not only has it encountered very little opposition, but in many postcommunist countries, public opinion polls show that constitutional courts enjoy high levels of popular support.[19]

Perhaps even more striking has been the rise, especially in new democracies, of independent agencies explicitly meant to be free of control by the politically responsive branches of government. These include such institutions as central banks, electoral commissions, human rights commissions, anticorruption bodies, ombudsmen, and the like.[20] The new prominence of agencies of this kind obviously reflects in part a suspicion of the people's elected representatives, a sense that they cannot be trusted to refrain from seeking personal or partisan advantage at the expense of the public good. But it also reflects a triumph of liberal ways of thinking, a sense that limiting the excesses of government and protecting individual rights are of greater concern than translating immediate popular sentiment into public policy. Another sign of this same tendency is the increased emphasis being given today by political practitioners and political scientists alike to such concerns as constitutionalism, the rule of law, institutional checks and balances, and accountability. One may say that they are rediscovering the wisdom of the *Federalist* papers, seeking protection against the dangerous tendencies of popular government through remedies that are themselves compatible with popular government. In fact, the popularity of the attack on illiberal democracy may itself be regarded as a sign of the triumph of liberalism.

For the most part, the response to Zakaria's critique has not taken the form of arguments depreciating the importance of such liberal desiderata as constitutionalism, the rule of law, and individual rights compared to that of popular elections. Virtually everyone joining the debate has agreed on the value of these liberal goals. The argument has instead focused on whether, in societies lacking a strong liberal tradition, authoritarian or elected government is a more promising road for achieving them. The real issue is whether the nineteenth-century sequence of first liberalism, then democracy, can work today, when the progress of liberal ideas has undermined traditional nondemocratic claims to political legitimacy.

It is worth noting that, in contrast to the current widespread experimentation with various kinds of checks and balances and independent agencies, there have been virtually no experiments with limited suffrage (at least in liberal, self-governing societies). If anything, the right to universal and equal suffrage is more unchallenged today than it has ever been, and it is hard to see on what acceptable grounds limitations on suffrage might be introduced. If there is little clamor for more populist government, there is none at all for exclusionary government. It is precisely the triumph of the liberal principle that all men are created equal that makes it virtually impossible for nondemocratic liberalism to flourish in the contemporary world. For better or worse, the future of liberalism is indissolubly tied to the future of liberal democracy.

III

LIBERAL DEMOCRACY AND
THE NATION-STATE

6

Globalization and Self-Government

2002

Two broad international trends have dominated the last quarter of the twentieth century and the initial years of the twenty-first: globalization and democratization. Although both globalization and democratization have long and complex histories, each was greatly accelerated by the collapse of Soviet communism in the revolutions of 1989–1991. These two trends have been interrelated and, for the most part, mutually reinforcing. That is to say, globalization has fostered democratization, and democratization has fostered globalization. Moreover, both trends generally have furthered American interests and contributed to the strengthening of American power. Yet while the impact of globalization on democracy has been largely positive until now, this will not necessarily be the case in the future. As the new century unfolds, globalization may come to pose a threat to democracy and a set of difficult dilemmas for the United States.

Globalization is probably the most prominent social science "buzzword" of our day, having recently wrested that distinction from the term "civil society." Having by now read literally dozens of attempts to fix a precise definition for "civil society," I have come to the conclusion that it is impossible to establish an exact, let alone consensual, meaning for such buzzwords. They simply are used and misused by too many different authors in too many different ways. On the other hand, if we are seriously to discuss the nature and potential consequences of globalization, it will hardly suffice to apply to it U.S. Supreme Court Justice Potter Stewart's famous pronouncement about obscenity: "I know it when I see it." So let me try briefly to elucidate the complex of meanings, mostly complementary but sometimes contradictory, that seems to be embodied in the term "globalization."

In the first place, as the word's root suggests, globalization refers to processes that are worldwide in scope. In this sense, it all started with Christopher Columbus, for prior to the discovery of the New World there were no truly global developments, at least in the political, social, or economic realms. But if globalization is understood solely or primarily in this "planetary" sense, then not just the discoveries and conquests of the early modern era, but the European imperialism of the nineteenth century and the world wars of the twentieth have been among its most potent instruments. The metaphor that best captures this meaning of globalization is that we live in "a *shrinking* world," one in which developments in any part of the world—whether for good or ill—are likely to impinge on people living elsewhere, sometimes with startling rapidity.

Of course, the shrinking of the world has given rise to global cooperation as well as global conflict. Some of today's international organizations, such as the International Telecommunication Union and the Universal Postal Union, date back well into the nineteenth century. Today there are a multiplicity of such organizations covering almost every aspect of international life. And of course, the United Nations itself, in which virtually every country in the world is represented by an ambassador in New York, constitutes a formal recognition of the global order.

A further consequence of the shrinking of the world is that peoples everywhere tend to become more alike. This too is an old story. In the middle of the eighteenth century, Jean-Jacques Rousseau wrote:

> To the extent that races are mixed and peoples confounded, one sees the gradual disappearance of those national differences which previously struck the observer at first glance. Formerly, each nation remained more closed in upon itself. There was less communication, less travel, fewer common or contrary interests, and fewer political and civil relations among peoples; there were . . . no regular or resident ambassadors; great voyages were rare; there was little far-flung commerce. . . . There is now a hundred times more contact between Europe and Asia than there formerly was between Gaul and Spain. Europe alone used to be more diverse than the whole world is today.[1]

Obviously, the tendency that Rousseau described has not only continued but accelerated over the past two and a half centuries. In recent decades, in fact, especially thanks to advances in communications technology, it has advanced so swiftly that the current degree of globalization may plausibly be regarded as constituting a difference in kind.

This brings us to the more expansive understanding of globalization put forward by champions of that combination of global markets and unfettered technological advance known as "the new economy" (at least that is what it was called during the heady days of the 1990s). This view is nicely captured in a full-page newspaper ad that was taken by the giant financial firm Merrill Lynch at the height of the international economic crisis in 1998. The ad, cited by Thomas Friedman in his colorful and deservedly popular 1999 book *The Lexus and the Olive Tree*, is headlined "The World Is 10 Years Old," and reads as follows:

> It was born when the Wall fell in 1989. It's no surprise that the world's youngest economy—the global economy—is still finding its bearings. . . . Many world markets are only recently freed, governed for the first time by the emotions of the people rather than the fists of the state. From where we sit, none of this diminishes the promise offered a decade ago by the demise of the walled-off world. . . . The spread of free markets and democracy around the world is permitting more people everywhere to turn their aspirations into achievements. And technology, properly harnessed and liberally distributed, has the power to erase not just geographical borders but also human ones.[2]

Understood in this way, globalization goes beyond more frequent and more intensive contact among peoples; it is a process of integration that draws together *individuals* living in different countries. In so doing, it makes national differences not only less sharp but also less consequential. For the enthusiasts of free markets and the Internet, economics and technology trump politics. As suggested by the Merrill Lynch ad, this view of globalization holds that it is creating a world where borders matter less and less, or an increasingly *borderless* world.

It would be hard to deny that technological advances, together with the current ascendancy of free markets and democracy, now make possible a degree of global commerce and "people-to-people" contacts that would have been unthinkable in earlier eras. The key questions that remain unanswered, however, are how persistent this tendency is and how far it will go toward eroding the significance of political boundaries. A shrinking world does not necessarily lead to a borderless world. To take just one example, the international Islamist terrorism that erupted most spectacularly on September 11, 2001, certainly provided dramatic evidence of globalization in the sense of a shrinking world. Yet at the same time it underlined how much territorial boundaries still matter, and global terrorist networks surely must be regarded as a major obstacle to globalization understood in the sense of a borderless world.

THE PROGRESS OF DEMOCRATIZATION

There is also, of course, considerable controversy about the meaning of democracy, though much less today than a couple of decades ago, when some still took seriously such notions as "people's democracy," "one-party democracy," or "revolutionary democracy." Current debate among political scientists is largely between those who adopt a minimalist definition tied solely to the holding of free elections and those who insist that a more ample degree of protection of political and civil liberties is also required. But whichever of these definitions one chooses, it is plain that the number of democracies in the world has soared since the "third wave" of democracy was launched with the Portuguese revolution of 1974.

In his now-classic 1991 book *The Third Wave: Democratization in the Late Twentieth Century,* Samuel P. Huntington, using a minimalist definition, wrote about how the number of democracies in the world nearly doubled between 1973 and 1990, going from thirty to fifty-eight.[3] Notwithstanding the endless controversy about how individual countries should be classified, there can be no denying that these numbers have risen markedly in the decade since his book appeared. According to Freedom House's assessment for 2001, the number of "electoral democracies" (countries who choose their leaders through free elections) is now 121, while the number of countries rated as Free in terms of safeguarding political rights and civil liberties is 86. These gains, it is true, occurred mainly in the early part of the 1990s and have now leveled off, and many new democracies remain troubled. Yet it is striking how rare have been the cases of outright reversion to authoritarianism—Pakistan is one of the few prominent examples—and how many significant democratic advances there have been over the last few years: the fall of dictators in Indonesia and Nigeria; the ouster of rulers hostile to democracy in Slovakia, Croatia, and Serbia; and the peaceful turnover of power to opposition leaders for the first time in Korea, Taiwan, Mexico, Senegal, and Ghana.

As discussed in previous chapters, this continuing democratic progress is partly attributable to the ideological supremacy of democracy. Amartya Sen, comparing the current global standing of democracy to a "default" setting in a computer program, states: "While democracy is not yet uniformly practiced, nor indeed universally accepted, in the general climate of world opinion democratic governance has now achieved the status of being taken to be generally right."[4] He notes that this represents a striking change from only a short time ago, when supporters of democracy in the developing countries were very much on the defensive. One might add that the survival even of weak and poorly functioning democracies has been greatly aided by the discrediting of military rule, one-party systems, and other authoritarian alternatives.

Over the past decade, the two doctrines that seemed to have the greatest potential for mounting an ideological challenge to liberal democracy have been Islamic fundamentalism and "Asian values." Although the events of September 11 reaffirmed that Islamic fundamentalism is capable of mobilizing fanatical resistance to democracy, it remains doubtful that it can become the basis for powerful modern states. In fact, Islamic fundamentalism appears to represent a less immediate threat to most Arab rulers today than it did a decade ago. And in the most important country where it has been in power, Iran, its grip is weakening. Especially striking is the extent to which many of those within the clerical regime itself, including former President Mohammad Khatami, have adopted the vocabulary of "civil society," the "rule of law," and the rights of citizens, while the public has grown increasingly anticlerical and prodemocratic.[5] Meanwhile, the appeal of "Asian values" has been weakened not only by the Asian financial crisis but by the fall of one of its most prominent exponents, former Indonesian dictator Suharto, and by the progress of democracy in such key Asian countries as Korea, Taiwan, and Thailand.[6] Neither of these doctrines can yet be counted out, but today they do not seem to pose a serious challenge to the ideological hegemony of democracy.

The unparalleled worldwide legitimacy of democracy can be seen in the recent evolution of international law and institutions.[7] While democracy also enjoyed a preeminent position following the Second World War—as is reflected in the inclusion in the Universal Declaration of Human Rights (1948) of Article 21, which spells out the right of all people to take part in government through free elections—the right to free elections tended to become a dead letter with the intensification of the Cold War and then the proliferation of one-party regimes. Since the fall of the Berlin Wall, however, it has been revived in all kinds of international charters, agreements, and declarations. Nor is this simply a matter of rhetoric. Support for democracy also has been embodied in the practices of numerous multilateral organizations, both global and regional. A wide variety of international bodies, as well as major Western governments, now provide "democracy assistance" in one form or another. Even the World Bank, under the label of "governance," often imposes a kind of "democratic conditionality" on its lending. Democracy is also increasingly a criterion for diplomatic recognition and membership in the most important regional organizations. And in the case of Haiti in 1994, the United Nations even passed a resolution justifying the use of force to restore to power an elected leader who had been ousted by a coup.

On the whole, then, there is little question that thus far globalization and the spread of democracy have been mutually reinforcing. In the first place, the domination of the world by a single ideology, almost whatever its content, is likely to be more favorable to globalization than a world that is divided into ideologically opposed blocs, as was the case during the bipolar order of the Cold War era. But beyond this, there are obvious affinities between globalization and democracy. Liberal democracy clearly favors the economic arrangements that foster globalization—namely, the market economy and an open international trading system. Moreover, liberal democracy's emphasis on the freedom of the individual and the right to information helps to promote the free flow of communications that has powered globalization. It is no accident that the countries that are seeking significant limits on the access of their citizens to the Internet are all non-democracies. Globalization, in turn, contributes to undermining authoritarian regimes by exposing their peoples to interaction with and information about other ways of life. It clearly gives an advantage to societies that are more open, flexible, and transparent, and thus, at least in the short run, it is favorable to democracy.

THE TWO SIDES OF LIBERAL DEMOCRACY

Why, then, do I suggest that over the longer run globalization and democracy may be at odds with each other? Answering this question requires that we be more precise about the nature and definition of democracy. When people speak of democracy today, they are referring not to the democracy of the ancient city but to modern liberal democracy. As I have argued earlier in this book, and as a number of other authors have emphasized in recent years, liberal democracy involves an uneasy marriage of two components—a liberal element that limits the scope and reach of government in the name of preserving individual freedom, and an element based on popular sovereignty that calls for majority rule, as expressed at the ballot box.[8] (This latter element can be called democratic in the strict sense, as it invokes the etymological meaning of the term—the rule of the people.) Without the liberal element, majority rule risks descending into the tyranny of a majority that may ride roughshod over the rights of individuals and minorities. And without the majoritarian element, there is a strong risk that unaccountable rulers pursuing their own selfish interests or ideological schemes will invade the rights of the citizenry.

The liberal element of liberal democracy has little difficulty in accommodating globalization. Liberalism is based on the natural rights and the desire for property and comfortable self-preservation that are equally possessed by all human beings. As such, it is universal in its reach, just as the principles of human rights and the laws of the market are universal. Liberalism limits the state in the name of the prepolitical or suprapolitical goals of the individual. In principle, there is no reason why a liberal order could not be administered by a wise and benevolent despot. Nor is there any reason why it could not be implemented by a universal world state as well as or better than by existing nation-states. If Americans and Canadians, or Frenchmen and Germans, have the same human rights, there seems to be no *liberal* reason why they should be separated by artificial borders and have different governments implement the protection of those rights. In this sense, liberalism is a wholly cosmopolitan doctrine that is in full harmony with the trend toward globalization.

The same is not true of the democratic or self-governing component of liberal democracy, which requires that the people be the ultimate authors of the laws that they must obey. That means the people must choose who will govern them, and that elected leaders must remain accountable to the people. This self-governing aspect of liberal democracy implies special bonds linking the members of the political community. They must be more than simply human beings bearing rights; they must be citizens who have special duties and obligations toward their fellow citizens. In practical terms, such citizenship is simply not possible on a global scale. While the idea of "world citizenship" may sound appealing in theory, it is very hard to imagine it working successfully in practice. Even apart from the vast diversity of languages, religions, and cultures that would have to be overcome to form a worldwide political community, the notion that a polity with six billion citizens could govern itself democratically seems utterly implausible.

There is something paradoxical about the way in which liberal democracies are able to combine adherence to universal principles with a powerful sense of loyalty and obligation to a particular polity. This is especially striking in the case of the United States, where the ties of citizenship are based less on common descent or nationality in the usual sense than on a fierce attachment to a constitutional order held to embody universal principles. A clue to this puzzling combination can be found in the doctrine of the social contract, as presented by the preeminent liberal political philosopher John Locke.

The basic premise of Locke's teaching is that human beings are "by nature, all free, equal, and independent," and therefore "no one can be . . . subjected to the political power of another, without his own consent." Thus the only basis for legitimate government is an agreement or contract among a number of people to unite into a political community. Such an agreement requires individuals to obligate themselves to accept the determination of the majority, for if the parties to the contract sought to retain their natural liberty no community could subsist. Any number of people may choose to unite in such a community, says Locke, "because it injures not the freedom of the rest; they are left as they were in the liberty of the state of nature." In fact, one of the chief reasons why people unite themselves into a community is to obtain "a greater security against any, that are not of it." What this theory entails is that liberty or rights are natural and hence universal; political obligations, by contrast, are conventional and are owed only to those with whom one enters into the social contract. Accordingly, to ensure that their universal human rights are protected, people must enroll themselves in a particular political order.[9]

THE GLOBAL ECONOMY VERSUS SELF-GOVERNMENT

To the extent that globalization tends to efface all barriers between countries and to remove effective decision making from the national level, it threatens to weaken not only authoritarian regimes but democratic ones as well. In fact, one may say that globalization, carried to its logical conclusion, is hostile to self-government as such. A borderless world is most unlikely to be a democratic one. Thus the preservation of democracy may well require certain limits on globalization.

There are already many signs of the emerging tension between globalization and democracy. The large-scale demonstrations against the WTO, the IMF, and the World Bank are, of course, one sign of this. Although the ideological agenda (or agendas) of the protesters does not enjoy wide political support, they do tap into real popular discontent over the fact that important developments and decisions seem to be increasingly beyond the influence of political leaders at the national level. To the extent that citizens, especially in smaller and less powerful countries, feel that their elected leaders have lost all power to govern the national economy or to preserve the national culture, democracy may be severely weakened. This danger cannot justify every short-sighted attempt at protectionism, but it is a very real problem. Globalization is likely to proceed whether we wish it to or not. But the form that globalization takes, and above all its relation to the autonomy of the nation-state (the home of modern liberal democracy), is a matter that is not wholly beyond our control.

The autonomy of the nation-state is potentially threatened both by the workings of global markets and by the rise of multilateral institutions. The first of these challenges takes the form of the triumph of economics over politics. The second would substitute a new set of global political institutions and allegiances for national ones. Let me say a word about each.

From the outset, modern liberal democracy has been identified with a substantial freeing up of the economic sphere. For Locke, "the great and chief end" for which men unite under government "is the preservation of their property." And while it is true that he sometimes uses the term property in a broader sense that includes men's "lives, liberty, and estates," it is also true that he places greater emphasis on the "secure enjoyment" and increase of material goods than any previous political thinker.[10] Thus at its very foundations, liberal democracy is bound up with a view that, while insisting on the indispensability of the political, in some sense puts it in the service of the economic.

Moreover, the liberal tradition has long understood commerce as an ally of liberty. This understanding is especially apparent in Montesquieu's treatment in *The Spirit of the Laws* of England, the country that he regards as the great model of liberty. Of the English, he even says that, unlike other peoples, they "have ever made their political interests give way to those of commerce." Moreover, in a chapter entitled "How Commerce Broke through the Barbarism of Europe," Montesquieu presents a fascinating account of how the development of international exchange forced medieval European rulers to limit their depredations of their subjects. Because the Church's condemnation of commerce had effectively restricted its practice to the Jews, many of the latter became wealthy. But the Jews were "pillaged by the tyranny of princes," who taxed them exorbitantly, tortured them to extort money, and expelled them so they could seize their properties. In response to their plight, Jewish merchants invented the bill of exchange. By this means, Montesquieu contends, "commerce . . . was able to elude violence and to maintain itself everywhere, as even the richest merchant now had only invisible wealth, which could be transferred anywhere without leaving any traces."[11] As a result, rulers had to learn to be more moderate and restrained if they did not want themselves and their countries to become impoverished.

One must acknowledge, then, that limiting the reach of government in order to allow the economic sphere to flourish is a long-standing feature of liberal thought and practice. But this in no way requires a dogmatic adherence in every case to unregulated commerce or free markets. Moreover, serious advocates of free markets, unlike some of the more overheated enthusiasts for globalization, understand the importance of political institutions for making free markets work effectively—a point that has been driven home by the checkered experience of market-oriented economic reform in the postcommunist world. There are no doubt lots of individual policy issues here in the United States where the influence of commercial interests seeking freer trade wrongly supersedes other domestic and foreign policy concerns, including national security. At the same time, commercial interests also frequently succeed in erecting protectionist trade barriers at the expense of other legitimate national interests.

On the whole, I do not believe that for the foreseeable future the increasing globalization of economic activity poses any threat to American democracy, in large part because the nation-state and the democratic accountability that it ensures are much more robust than the economic globalizers may realize. There is no question that the problem is potentially more serious for newer and poorer democracies, but successful economic growth is likely to take much of the sting out of limitations on their policy choices. And for those countries whose economies are unsuccessful, democracy is bound to be precarious in any case.

GLOBAL INSTITUTIONS VERSUS SELF-GOVERNMENT

The rise of multilateral institutions is a natural response to a shrinking world. As cross-border contacts multiply, both in the economy and in other spheres, there is an inevitable need for institutions that can address problems that lie beyond the competence of any single state. Even for a superpower like the United States, neither isolationism nor across-the-board unilateralism is a realistic option. The serious argument is about the nature of multilateral institutions and their powers vis-à-vis national governments.

In the years ahead, I believe that this will become an increasingly contentious issue, one that may well lead to unusual political divisions and alignments. For example, even those who have been strong proponents of policies to promote the global spread of democracy are likely to split into two camps, dividing those who wish to see a world of democratically governed nation-states from those who wish to see a democratic world community—those who are concerned with preserving the sovereignty of democratic nations from those who favor the universalization not only of markets but also of politics and law. In short, we will see a split between those committed to the democratic component of liberal democracy and those emphasizing its liberal component.

Signs of the conflict within prodemocracy ranks between "liberals" and "democrats" are perhaps most visible today with regard to the issue of punishment for human rights violations. In the case of the attempt by a Spanish judge to extradite former Chilean dictator Augusto Pinochet or the effort to bring Slobodan Milošević to trial before the International Criminal Tribunal for Yugoslavia in the Hague, "liberals" have generally favored international legal action against such human rights abusers, while many "democrats" in Chile and Yugoslavia, respectively (as well as some of their supporters abroad), have worried about the damaging effects that this might have on building stable democracy at home. The concerns of the "democrats" include not only considerations of national sovereignty and the possibility that widely publicized international trials might inflame internal divisions and make more difficult the process of national reconciliation, but also the fear that failure to grapple with such matters domestically would retard the needed strengthening of democratic political and judicial institutions. In the United States, of course, we have seen a somewhat similar division of opinion regarding the new International Criminal Court, as well as policies toward other international agencies and instruments that are seen as infringing on American sovereignty.

Another arena for this same conflict is the debate over the future of the European Union. Strictly speaking, of course, the European Union is a regional rather than a worldwide institution, but it is at the same time the clearest example we have today of an effort at integrating sovereign national states. As Ralf Dahrendorf put it in a recent article, "Many . . . see the institutional Europe as a step toward coping with globalization by democratic means. If we cannot have global democracy just yet, we can at least begin the journey to that goal by creating a large world region, Europe, along democratic principles."[12]

The European Union has in many ways been a liberal project par excellence. Yet while it has achieved notable success in building a common market and a consensus on human rights, the European Union is now widely acknowledged to be suffering from a "democratic deficit."[13] This complaint was initially made by critics who wanted to reinforce the power of democratically elected national parliaments vis-à-vis Brussels, but it has subsequently been picked up by proponents of more thoroughgoing integration who wish to enhance the legitimacy of European institutions. What this suggests is that the European Union has arrived at an awkward in-between position: It has too much authority to be able to rest its democratic credentials solely on the internal democratic institutions of its member states, but its member states are unwilling truly to democratize the EU because they know that this would imply an irreversible loss of their own national sovereignty.

Currently, a European convention, chaired by former French president Valéry Giscard d'Estaing, has been convened to address the future of the EU. Some have likened this to the Philadelphia convention of 1787 that drafted the U.S. Constitution and succeeded in uniting the thirteen colonies to form a new state with its own democratic institutions. There is no reason in principle that the Europeans could not do the same, but there is every reason in practice to assume that they will not, for the countries of the old continent do not appear to be willing to subsume themselves in their new creation. As an article in *Le Figaro* reported, recently reelected French president Jacques Chirac sought, in a campaign speech on 6 March 2002, "to square the circle," promising "to build a Europe powerful in the world while at the same time preserving the identity of the French nation."[14] According to the report, Chirac "advocated enhanced European integration but also posed limits to it: no European superstate and no United States of Europe." Although Chirac himself acknowledged the EU's "deficit of democratic legitimacy" and proposed some reforms to help repair it, it is difficult to imagine how the EU could be genuinely democratized without undermining the sovereignty of its member states.

GLOBALIZATION AND THE UNITED STATES

The question of how the United States fits into the overall picture that I have sketched is a complex one. One useful way of approaching it is by distinguishing between the liberal and democratic strands in the American fabric. These two sometimes conflicting tendencies (one liberal and universalist, the other democratic and nationalist) often make the United States seem schizophrenic in its attitude toward the rest of the world. On the one hand, as a liberal, open, and exceedingly diverse society explicitly founded upon universal principles, the United States is better equipped than most other countries to adapt to and profit from globalization. With economic interests in every corner of the globe, the United States stands to benefit from developments that promote international cooperation and harmonization on an ever greater scale. Thus it has a strong bent toward multilateralism and support for international law and regulation. On the other hand, among advanced democracies it is in the United States where jealousy about national sovereignty (in the political rather than the economic or cultural realm) seems most acute, prompting it toward the unilateralism so many other nations complain of today. The democratic component of liberal democracy remains especially strong in this country, and thus some aspects of globalization run into strong opposition in the United States, opposition that is likely to grow.

Before elaborating upon this analysis, it is worth emphasizing that the international order that sustains globalization is underpinned by American military predominance. In the words of the French diplomat and author Jean-Marie Guéhenno (now Under-Secretary-General of the United Nations for Peacekeeping Operations), "the apolitical world of globalization can prosper only under the aegis of a political entity, its guarantor, the United States."[15] As the events of September 11 underlined, there are significant forces in the world hostile to the current order, and they cannot be kept in check solely by economic superiority or other forms of "soft power." Territory and the ability to defend it still remain ultimately decisive.

At the same time, it is now widely, and often bitterly, acknowledged that America towers over other nations not only in military strength but in economic might and in cultural influence. Observers elsewhere often attribute America's unilateralist tendencies to its disproportionate power, and some in this country see efforts to restrain the United States through multilateral institutions as an effort by Lilliputians to tie down the American Gulliver. No doubt this way of viewing things is not wholly devoid of foundation, but there is also much that it does not explain. In particular, it would be hard to square such an explanation with U.S. behavior after the Second World War, when America also enjoyed a great preponderance of power yet devoted itself to establishing the array of multilateral bodies that constitute the institutional architecture of globalization to this day.

What is it about the United States that has enabled it to prosper in the era of globalization? In *The Lexus and the Olive Tree*, Thomas Friedman suggests a thought experiment: If in 1900 a "visionary geo-architect" had been told about the coming of globalization a century hence, "what sort of country would he have designed to compete and to win in that world?" Friedman's answer is that this visionary "would have designed something that looks an awful lot like the United States."[16] He then goes on to enumerate various aspects of America that equip it to excel in the age of globalization—including its geographical position; its diverse population and openness to immigrants; its economic dynamism and entrepreneurial spirit; its flexible, honest, and transparent legal system; its tolerance and individualism; its commitment to the free flow of information. This is generally accurate as far as it goes, but it does not seem to me to capture the full picture. For while it explains much of what has enabled America to seize the opportunities offered by globalization, it fails to explain what has enabled America to resist its dangers.

Guéhenno, in the essay quoted above, offers some interesting reflections on this question. Noting that globalization is increasingly regarded as a synonym for Americanization, he explores how Washington, despite the American people's preoccupation with domestic matters and lack of interest in foreign affairs, has "almost unwittingly" become the capital of what the rest of the world views as an empire. Guéhenno explains the envy and resentment with which the United States is viewed as follows: "What fascinates and irks at the same time is the way in which Americans can reduce politics to a clash of interests, and yet maintain the vitality of the American polity. How can one reconcile the fact of globalization, which ignores borders and destroys the old social structures that mediate between the individual and the global marketplace, with this other reality, the American nation, which seems to resist globalization better than most communities."[17]

Guéhenno answers his question by citing America's "institutional" patriotism, the fact that it views itself as "a community of choice, built upon a contract," which he contrasts with other nations that see their own communities as built "on more than functional choices." I think that this points us in the right direction, but that in emphasizing solely the functional or "utilitarian" character of Americans' devotion to their country, Guéhenno pushes his argument too far. An Eastern European friend of mine once remarked that Americans always think of themselves as representing what is new and changing in the world. In his view, however, the American polity is most importantly a model of tradition and stability, with the continuity of its more than two hundred-year-old regime, its veneration of its Founding Fathers and of its national monuments and symbols, and its civic spirit. It is America's profound attachment to its Constitution and its political traditions, I believe, that shields it against the potential threats posed by globalization.

This democratic or civic element also inevitably makes Americans jealous of their national sovereignty and unwilling to countenance any policies that would diminish the authority or reach of their Constitution. This may sometimes lead to a parochialism that fits poorly with America's outward-looking and liberal spirit and its leadership role in the world. But this is a tension that cannot be entirely resolved. What is needed, not only in America but in all liberal democracies, is to maintain a proper balance between their liberal and democratic elements. In most newer democracies, it is the liberal element that is weakest and most in need of reinforcement. In most advanced democracies, however, the situation is the reverse. And since the tendency of globalization is to favor liberalism at the expense of democracy, wise statesmen should not neglect the task of strengthening the common bonds of citizenship that are essential to a liberal democratic order.

7

Understanding the European Union

2003

Why, even during a period marked by a seemingly momentous debate over the adoption of a new constitution, do European publics show relatively little interest in the future political course of the European Union (EU)? And why is it so difficult to get non-Europeans interested in the politics of the EU?

This indifference is especially puzzling because the rebuilding of Western European societies upon the ashes of World War II and their subsequent achievement of peace, prosperity, and democracy surely constitute one of the great political success stories in modern history. Since the end of the Cold War, that success has been crowned by its extension to Central Europe, a development that was affirmed by the formal accession to the EU in May 2004 of eight postcommunist countries. Most observers would argue that the EU has been not just a symbol but a key instrument of these accomplishments. Moreover, the EU seems to represent an unprecedented success in forging a binding association among sovereign states, states that are among the oldest and most deeply rooted in the world, and that have a long history of fratricidal conflict.

The answer to the questions with which we began—as to almost all questions about the EU—is ambiguous. Most citizens in member and candidate countries alike surely want their homelands to be part of the EU, but they do not regard the EU as their homeland. Their attachment to it seems to be based much more on interest than on passion. Jacques Rupnik has noted the paradox that East-Central Europeans have tended to perceive NATO as a more "value-infused" institution than the EU, with the latter "seen as primarily an economic institution with complicated bureaucratic procedures."[1] And German foreign minister Joschka Fischer, in a far-reaching and

influential speech on the EU in May 2000, noted that the "process of European integration . . . is now being called into question by many people; it
is viewed as a bureaucratic affair run by a faceless, soulless Eurocracy in
Brussels—at best boring, at worst dangerous."[2]

One reason why the EU is often perceived in this manner may be found
in the way in which it has developed. Fischer speaks of European integration as having been based on the "Monnet method," named after Jean
Monnet, the French civil servant credited with being the Founding Father of
European union. This method, often identified with the social science theory known as "functionalism," favored promoting economic integration in
specific sectors, with the notion that this would produce "spillovers" into
other sectors and eventually create both the need and the momentum for
political integration. A salient aspect of this approach is that it not only
moved by gradual steps but eschewed any clear statement of what the end
product (or "finality") of integration would look like. The Monnet method,
sometimes characterized as "integration by stealth," tended to be favored
even by many enthusiasts of European political unification once it became
clear that European parliaments and publics were unlikely to support
bolder measures.

One result of the success of this approach is that for a long time there was
relatively little open political debate about the ultimate goals and shape of
the EU—a situation that Fischer's speech was intended to remedy. Indeed,
European integration is often conceived as an ongoing and open-ended
process rather than a purposeful movement toward a desired end. This explains why proponents of the EU are so concerned about maintaining its
forward momentum. A much-used simile suggests that the process of European integration is like riding a bike—unless you keep moving forward, you
will fall off. Even Fischer, who contends that the Monnet method has now
outlived its usefulness and calls for confronting the question of "finality,"
holds that the alternative facing Europe is "erosion or integration."

Because European integration has been viewed as a journey rather than a
destination, there is enormous ambiguity about precisely where it is heading. Thus the EU means very different things to different people:

- An institutional framework for assuring peace among the member states
- A way to recover the clout in international affairs that the major Euro-
  pean powers once wielded individually
- An essentially economic arrangement to build a large European market
- A vehicle for making European economies and firms more competitive
  with those of Asia and the United States
- A tool for countering U.S. political and cultural hegemony
- A practical response to the increasingly transnational dimension of the
  problems facing European states

- A first step toward global governance
- An instrument for forging a common European culture
- A framework for protecting and fostering cultural diversity, both within and among the states of Europe

There is also a lively debate about the nature of the beast. Some insist that, for all its supranationalist trappings, the EU is properly understood as an essentially intergovernmental institution that serves the interests of its member states. Others assert that it has already gone well beyond intergovernmentalism and is properly understood as the germ of an emerging European federal state. Still others argue that the EU is pursuing a course that combines elements of both intergovernmentalism and federalism, though it is often unclear whether this is understood as a stable middle ground or merely a stopping point on the long path toward a federal state. Meanwhile, a number of academic theorists contend that the EU is a new kind of political entity altogether, one that cannot be located on the state-based continuum running from intergovernmentalism to federalism. They variously characterize it instead as a "neomedieval" or "postmodern" or "post-state" or "non-state" polity.

As if the ambiguous nature of the EU and the uncertainty about its goals did not complicate matters enough, those who seek to understand it must also grapple with the arcane language employed in discussions of European integration. Not only does the EU boast the long list of acronyms typical of all international organizations, but it also has given rise to a host of specialized terms (in various languages) that are often unintelligible to outsiders—and perhaps to many Europeans as well. The goal of this chapter is to help make the terms of the debate on European integration more intelligible to nonspecialists, to provide some of the basic historical and institutional background necessary for understanding it, and to elucidate some of the critical issues that it raises. Among the latter are some very fundamental questions about the nature of democracy, and it is with a discussion of these that this chapter will conclude.

THE FIRST DECADES

Although the idea of European integration is an old one, the first serious attempts to realize it in practice were a product of the situation following World War II. The imperative of postwar economic recovery, especially in the face of a growing Soviet threat to Western Europe, entailed the need for building a strong West Germany, but the prospect of German resurgence understandably worried the French. Hence the need for an institutional framework that would bind together Germany and France, whose rivalry had long been the flashpoint of intra-European conflict. The first crucial step toward implementing such a framework was the 1950 Schuman Plan (proposed by French foreign minister Robert Schuman and masterminded by Jean Monnet), which led to the establishment in 1952 of the European Coal and Steel Community (ECSC). This was a supranational organization, composed of France, Germany, Italy, and the Benelux countries, whose High Authority (initially headed by Jean Monnet) was charged with controlling the development of these critical industries.

The next major effort toward European integration was made in the field of defense. After the outbreak of the Korean War, Western nations felt that it was necessary to rearm West Germany. The French proposed the establishment of a European Defense Community (EDC), within the framework of NATO, that would fuse a portion of the armed forces and equipment of the EDC member states. This too was meant to be a supranational organization, one that would be governed by a European Political Community. Although the same six states that formed the ECSC signed the EDC treaty in 1952, the latter's ratification was defeated in the French National Assembly in 1954, and both the EDC and the European Political Community failed to come into being. Thereafter, steps toward European integration were essentially confined to the economic sphere.

Monnet was again instrumental in the launching of the European Atomic Energy Community (EURATOM), modeled on the ECSC. More significant, however, was a plan for a broader economic community that would eliminate tariffs between member states, forge a unified trade policy toward the rest of the world, and devise common policies on a range of economic issues. Both this proposal for a European Economic Community (EEC) and EURATOM were approved in separate treaties signed in Rome in 1957. Nonetheless, it is the founding document of the EEC that is generally referred to as the Treaty of Rome and has been considered the legal cornerstone of European integration. Eschewing the more explicitly supranational language of some of the earlier treaties, the Treaty of Rome calls for laying "the foundations of an ever closer union of the peoples of Europe."

During the following decade, the European Economic Community (which commonly became referred to simply as the European Community, or EC) made substantial progress toward achieving a common market and flourished economically, but there were no major new institutional developments. During the 1960s, the British, who had earlier held aloof from efforts at European integration, twice applied for EC membership, but were effectively vetoed by French president Charles de Gaulle in 1963 and again in 1967. A firm opponent of supranationalism, de Gaulle also successfully battled against efforts by EC governing organs to enhance their powers. It was not until 1972 that Britain, along with Denmark and Ireland, was finally admitted. (Norway, whose application for membership was also accepted, saw its entry voted down in a popular referendum.) Otherwise, however, the 1970s were generally considered a period of "Eurosclerosis" or "Europessimism," in part due to the economic crisis launched by OPEC's oil-price hike in 1973 and the difficulties in assimilating Britain, which demanded a renegotiation of its terms of entry.

In the 1980s, the EC once again expanded, admitting Greece to membership in 1981 and Spain and Portugal in 1986. It is generally acknowledged that bringing into the fold these three southern European countries, all of whom had exited from authoritarianism in the mid–1970s, played a critical role in keeping them on the path toward democratic consolidation. A major structural reform of the EC occurred in 1986 with the signing of the Single European Act, which aimed at eliminating the barriers that still remained to the free movement of goods, services, capital, and people within the EC. It also increased the number of issues subject to qualified majority voting rather than unanimity, extended the competence of the Community in a variety of ways, and contained an agreement that the member states would "formulate and implement a European foreign policy."

THE MAASTRICHT TREATY AND ITS AFTERMATH

The most important constitutional change in the history of the EC came with the signing of the Treaty on European Union (TEU) in 1992, which formally subsumed the EC within a larger body called the European Union. Commonly known as the Maastricht Treaty, after the southern Dutch city in which it was signed, it is an enormously long and complex document that includes numerous amendments to the Treaty of Rome. In addition to approving a European Economic and Monetary Union (EMU), Maastricht fashioned a structure of three "pillars" that form the basis of the EU. The first pillar, which deals primarily with the economic sphere, consists of the EC; the second is the Common Security and Foreign Policy (CSFP); and the third is Cooperation on Justice and Home Affairs (JHA), which concerns such issues as asylum, immigration, cross-border problems, and police and judicial coordination. The Treaty also affirmed the concept of EU citizenship for all nationals of member states, giving them the freedom to move and to live anywhere in the EU and granting them certain rights. And it enshrined the somewhat vague concept of "subsidiarity," stating that "the Community shall take action, in accordance with the principle of subsidiarity, only if and in so far as the objectives of the proposed action cannot be sufficiently achieved by the Member States."

Although almost all the elements of Maastricht had been the object of a long history of prior negotiations, the outcome was also shaped by the dramatic world events of 1989–1991. The demise of communism in Eastern

Europe and the reunification of Germany in 1990 changed the political landscape of the continent. France was wary of German unification, but when it seemed inevitable, it sought to bind Germany as firmly as possible to Europe. At the same time, France was eager to achieve monetary union as a way to dilute the dominance of the Deutschmark. And Germany was willing to yield some of its monetary preeminence in return for entrenching a reunified Germany within European structures. The move toward a single currency embodied in the EMU was the most important outcome of Maastricht, though the price of its approval was a provision allowing Britain to "opt out" of adopting the euro, as it has thus far chosen to do.

The Maastricht Treaty ran into unexpected difficulties in the ratification process. Danish voters initially rejected it in June 1992, but after an agreement was reached allowing Denmark to opt out of various of its provisions, including the euro, Danish voters approved it the following year. Moreover, the treaty barely escaped defeat in France, with just 51 percent of the electorate voting in favor. The lack of popular enthusiasm revealed by the ratification process stirred great concern about the distance of EU institutions and processes from the European public and led to increasing discussion about how to repair what came to be widely called the EU's "democratic deficit." The 1990s also witnessed a good deal of debate about the twin goals of "widening" and "deepening" the EU, and the extent to which they were complementary or in tension with each other. That is, some worried that expanding to include countries from the postcommunist East would make it more difficult to forge the closer integration sought by many of the long-standing "core" members.

With the end of the Cold War, Western European states that had pursued neutralist foreign policies applied for EU membership. In 1995, Austria, Sweden, and Finland joined, bringing the twelve to fifteen. In Switzerland, however, and for a second time in Norway, voters rejected accession, and these remain the only two continental states in Western Europe still outside the EU. The bringing in of the poorer new democracies of the former Soviet bloc posed a much greater challenge. At the same time, both moral and geopolitical reasons seemed to make expansion to the east imperative. Eventually, the sentiment in favor of enlargement prevailed, but not a consensus to allow widening to come at the expense of deepening. Those favoring looser integration hoped that the inclusion of so many new countries would make deepening impracticable. On the other hand, some who favored closer integration hoped that the addition of the new members would make the unwieldiness of the existing governing machinery intolerable, and thus spur further deepening.

Though it proceeded more slowly than the candidate countries might have liked, enlargement did go forward, and in December 2002 the EU formally approved the accession of ten new member states—the Czech Republic, Estonia, Hungary, Latvia, Lithuania, Poland, Slovakia, and Slovenia, as well as the two small Mediterranean island states of Cyprus and Malta. The admitted states had to meet a series of stringent conditions and incorporate into their laws the so-called *acquis communautaire*, a host of rights and obligations deriving from various EU treaties and regulations that reputedly runs to more than eighty thousand pages. The candidate countries have been holding referenda on accession, so far approving it by wide margins (except in Malta, where the vote was close). There seems to be general agreement that EU membership will provide them with a road to democratic consolidation and economic progress. At the same time, there is considerable worry that enlargement will hurt those postcommunist countries that have not made the cut, weakening their prospects for democratic consolidation and economic progress.

The prospect of enlargement did indeed give rise to an enhanced focus on reforming the EU's institutional structure and machinery. This concern is evident in Fischer's speech, which notes that EU institutions, originally created for six member states, "just about still function with fifteen," and risk being "hopelessly overload[ed]" with twenty-five or more. Although some modest reforms were taken in the Amsterdam Treaty of 1997 and later in the Nice Treaty of 2001, these were widely regarded as insufficient. Spurred by the debate launched by Fischer's speech, European leaders concluded that a more fundamental restructuring was needed, and in December 2001 they issued the Laeken Declaration on the Future of the European Union.

The Laeken Declaration stated that "the Union stands at a crossroads," emphasizing in particular "the democratic challenge facing Europe" and the need to bring the Union's institutions "closer to its citizens." Toward this end, the document called for the convening of "a Convention composed of the main parties involved in the debate on the future of the Union." The document indicated that the Convention would be charged, at a minimum, with simplifying and reorganizing the existing EU treaties, but also pointedly raised the question of whether "this might not lead in the long run to the adoption of a constitutional text in the Union." Chaired by former French president Valéry Giscard d'Estaing, this Convention met in Brussels from February 2002 until July 2003, and its final document will be the basis for deliberations at an Intergovernmental Conference in Rome in October 2003.

INSTITUTIONS AND POLICIES

The institutional structure of the EU does not conveniently fit the division into three branches of government that is characteristic of democratic constitutional states. In fact, the Brussels-based European Commission, the most active and distinctive EU institution, combines executive and legislative functions, as well as serving as the Union's bureaucracy. For alongside its role of implementing community laws and policies, it has responsibility for proposing and developing them in the first place. The Commission currently consists of twenty members (two each from the larger states and one each from the rest) who function somewhat like cabinet ministers, with each taking charge of a particular portfolio. The commissioners are appointed by their national governments in consultation with the Commission president, but they must also be acceptable to the European Parliament (EP), which cannot reject individual appointments but can refuse to approve the entire slate. Commissioners cannot be removed by their national governments in midterm, and they must take an oath renouncing any defense of national interests. The Commission has the most supranational orientation of the EU governing organs, and it has played a key role in advancing integration, especially when led by a strong and assertive Commission president like Jacques Delors (1985–1994).

The most powerful legislative body of the EU is the Council of Ministers (now officially known as the Council of the European Union), which has the final say as to whether measures proposed by the Commission will become EU law or policy (though on some issues the European Parliament has a say as well). The Council, which meets in closed session, comprises the national ministers of the member states with responsibility for the issue under review (for instance, transport ministers for transportation issues), with the relevant European commissioner attending. Much of the Council's day-to-day work is carried out on its behalf by the Brussels-based Committee of Permanent Representatives (COREPER) of the member states. The Council does have a supranational element, in that on some issues decisions may be taken by a majority or qualified majority vote, but this applies only to the EU's "first pillar." For the second (foreign policy) and third (justice and home affairs) pillars, decisions can only be taken unanimously. The Council is chaired and guided by a presidency that rotates among the member states every six months. Thus Denmark occupied the Council presidency during the second half of 2002, Greece occupied it during the first half of 2003, and Italy during the second half of 2003.

Closely related to the Council of the European Union is the European Council (yes, it is a different body), which is composed of the heads of state and government of the member states, along with the president of the Commission. The European Council holds at least one "summit" meeting, hosted by the country that holds the presidency, during each six-month period. Although it has a rather slim legal basis in the EU treaties, it is able, thanks to the high level of its representatives, to exert a profound influence in shaping the agenda and the political direction of the EU.

The only directly elected and the most open of the major EU institutions, the European Parliament (EP), is also the least powerful. Although it began as an advisory body, the Parliament has gradually been expanding the areas in which it can exercise real influence, including the budget. Yet it is still widely regarded as not much more than a forum for debate, and the low level of popular interest in its work is reflected in low turnouts for EP elections, which are held every five years and typically revolve around national rather than European issues. Elections are organized on a national basis, with the size of each country's delegation weighted according to its population, but with smaller states enjoying proportionally greater representation. Plenary sessions of the 626-member Parliament meet for a few days each month in Strasbourg, France, but its committees meet in Brussels and its secretariat is divided between Luxembourg and Brussels. EP candidates are generally nominated by their national parties, and while parliamentarians group along party lines to some extent within the EP, real Europe-wide parties have not emerged.

The European Court of Justice (ECJ), a fifteen-member body based in Luxembourg, has been one of the leading engines of European integration. Judges are appointed for renewable six-year terms, and in practice one judge is selected by each member state. Although the Treaty of Rome gave the court little authority, it greatly expanded its influence through two key decisions that it issued in the early 1960s. One of these established the doctrine of "direct effect," which holds that EU law "produces direct effects and creates individual rights which national courts must protect." The second established the primacy of EU law over national law. As a result, decisions of the ECJ can have far-reaching effects on the laws and policies of EU member states. It is sometimes said that in this way the ECJ has succeeded in "constitutionalizing" the intergovernmental treaties that form the basis of EU law. Although national courts and public officials have sometimes complained about the reach of the ECJ, on the whole it has been remarkably successful in gaining compliance with its decisions.

Even in a description of the EU as brief as this one necessarily must be, a few words should be said about some of its most prominent policies and programs:

No doubt the most dramatic advance toward European integration in recent years has been the single currency now adopted by the twelve member states that have joined the European Monetary Union (EMU). An independent European Central Bank based in Frankfurt, Germany, with an executive board appointed by the European Council, now has exclusive responsibility for determining and implementing monetary policy. In order to become eligible for the EMU, countries that wished to join needed to meet a set of "convergence criteria" regarding their inflation rates, budget deficits, and interest rates. And having become part of the "euro zone," they are required by the Stability and Growth Pact to keep their budget deficits below 3 percent of GDP. Although this target has been missed by several countries recently, it is not clear how stringently adherence to it by EMU members will be enforced.

The Common Agricultural Policy (CAP) has been one of the EU's most controversial activities since the basis for it was written into the Treaty of Rome, partly as a means of securing French ratification. The form that the CAP took in the 1960s featured price supports for EU farmers and protectionism vis-à-vis agricultural imports from outside the EU. The result was a great increase in agricultural production, but also a drain on EU funds, with payments under CAP still amounting to almost half the EU budget. Numerous attempts to reform the CAP have been made over the years, but progress has been limited, and the CAP remains a source of frustration to many member states.

Another significant share of spending is absorbed by "structural funds" intended to aid poorer regions and countries within the EU. Funds for these purposes were markedly increased in the 1980s in order to compensate poorer countries for the costs of adjusting to the single market and to promote greater "cohesion" between richer northern Europe and the recent entrants from the south. These funds are generally thought to have contributed significantly to the economic gains achieved by Greece, Spain, and Portugal, as well as Ireland. Enlargement will bring ten new and much poorer claimants on these funds into the EU, and it is clear that the newcomers will not receive benefits on the scale previously enjoyed by the southern European countries.

Finally, mention should be made of the Schengen Agreement, named after the small town in Luxembourg in which five EU members first negotiated it in 1985. Since then the agreement has been expanded to include more countries and has been incorporated into the EU treaties (though Britain and Ireland have been permitted to opt out). Schengen calls for the free movement of persons within EU borders, but correspondingly mandates the hardening of controls at the Union's external borders (often referred to as "Schengen borders"). This is a source of great concern to the postcommunist countries, for it will require the erecting of hard borders to separate new EU members (like Poland) from nearby countries with which they have close ties (like Ukraine).

IDENTIFYING THE BEAST

So what kind of animal is the EU? An intergovernmental organization? An emerging federal state? Something in between? Or something altogether different? Each answer has a certain plausibility and is given by serious people.

Those who claim that the EU remains essentially an intergovernmental organization controlled by its member states have much evidence to cite on their behalf. The EU does not have either an army or a police force. If one accepts John Locke's definition of "political power" as including the right of making laws and "of employing the force of the community in the execution of such laws and in the defense of the commonwealth from foreign injury," then the EU wholly lacks political power. It is not in this sense a commonwealth or any other sort of state. Ultimate decision-making power on the most important matters rests with the governments of the member states. The EU has been least successful—as the crisis over the Iraq war recently demonstrated once again—in the effort to forge a common foreign and security policy. Unlike most associations of states in history, it has fared much better at harmonizing internal policies than external ones. Moreover, there is no real "European public space." The peoples of the EU speak many different languages. Their media, their party systems, and their politics as a whole are essentially national. A common argument holds that there is no European *demos,* and hence the EU cannot be a real democracy. Finally, EU revenues are strictly limited to less than 1.3 percent of GDP, compared to average governmental expenditures by the member states in the range of 40 percent.

Yet there is also strong evidence on the side of those who claim that the EU has gone well beyond the confines of an intergovernmental organization. It now has a common currency (at least for most of its members), and the coining of money has often been regarded as a mark of sovereignty. Most important of all, thanks to the decisions of the European Court of Justice cited above, EU law enjoys supremacy over national laws, and its reach extends to individuals within member states. And it is precisely the distinction between authority only over states and authority over individuals that the *Federalist* defines as the "characteristic difference between a league and a government." Finally, the EU's involvement in the regulation of almost all areas of economic activity means that decisions made in Brussels have a significant impact on the daily lives of Europeans.

It could be argued, of course, that what has been achieved so far are merely partial steps along the path toward a true federation of Europe. Yet support for a real European federal state appears to be waning rather than growing. Fischer's speech seemed to be pointing in this direction, but it was filled with ambiguity, insisting that even in the "fully sovereign" and "finalised Federation, the nation-state, with its cultural and democratic traditions, will be irreplaceable in ensuring the legitimation of a union of citizens and states that is wholly accepted by the people." In speeches in some measure responding to Fischer's, France's Jacques Chirac and Britain's Tony Blair emphasized even more strongly the primacy of the European nations. Chirac told the German Bundestag: "Neither you nor we are envisaging the creation of a super European State which would supplant our national states and mark the end of their existence as players in international life."[3] And Blair, in a speech at the Polish Stock Exchange, concluded: "We need to get the political foundations of the European Union right. These foundations are rooted in the democratic nation state."[4] Yet both Chirac and Blair also noted approvingly those aspects of the EU that involve a "pooled" or "common sovereignty." They do not seem to see any contradiction in this halfway house between intergovernmentalism and supranationalism.

There does indeed appear to be a sense among most Europeans concerned with these issues that both the traditional intergovernmentalist approach and the traditional federalist approach are now equally outmoded. Blair argues that this reflects the wishes of the European people, who want an EU that is much more than just a free-trade area but much less than a federal state. No doubt that is the wish of many Europeans, but the people may often have contradictory wishes (e.g., low levels of taxation along with high levels of public services). The question is how stable the compromise between intergovernmentalism and federalism currently embodied in the EU really is. While it may violate long-held notions of political theory,[5] it cannot be denied that it survives and it functions. There may be reason to doubt, however, how well it would hold up in the face of an economic or a military crisis.

One way of resolving (or skirting) the potential conflict between EU sovereignty and nation-state sovereignty is to question or downgrade the notion of sovereignty altogether. This is the route taken by many academic specialists on the EU. They argue that in an age of globalization the nation-state is losing its centrality and its ability to deal with the social and economic challenges confronting it. This is not simply a matter of scale, and therefore constructing a continental European state will not solve it. The proponents of this outlook tend to see the current era as marking a historical watershed, bringing to an end several hundred years during which the nation-state was the dominant actor on the world scene. Thus they are fond of using such terms as postmodern, postnational, or post-Westphalian to refer to the new formations that they see emerging. Others speak favorably of the EU as following a "neomedieval" model or even as marking a kind of reemergence of the Holy Roman Empire. What they have in mind in using these terms is a political order characterized not by exclusive territorial rule but by multiple allegiances and overlapping jurisdictions.

Yet they do not envisage a return to the widespread disorder and use of force that marked the feudal period. Instead, they see the waning power of the nation-state as yielding to the transnational rule of law on a previously unprecedented scale. In European academic circles, at least, multilateralism in all its forms occupies the moral high ground, and national interests and outlooks are generally regarded as retrograde. The problem of enforcing the law receives relatively little attention. Perhaps this is not surprising, given that the decisions of the EU, and especially its Court of Justice, have met with a remarkable degree of compliance, despite the EU's inability to enforce them.

It is questionable, however, whether this "non-state" model of the EU can deliver all that Europeans want. For among the many other motives pushing toward integration is the desire of Europeans to be a major player on the world scene. Some may hold that this can be achieved wholly through "soft power"—that is, the power of the European example in pointing toward a world governed by multilateralism and the rule of law. Others, however, want the EU to have a more muscular role. Both Chirac and Blair in the speeches cited above emphasize that they seek a Europe that will be a "world power" or a "superpower but not a superstate." Of course, France and Britain are the only two EU members that spend a significant share of their GDP on defense, and this view is not necessarily shared by most Europeans. Indeed, many of them would prefer an EU whose world role resembled that of a huge NGO. And to make matters even more complicated, there are others who are attracted to the idea of a non-state EU because they believe that NATO should remain the central security institution of Europe.

THE QUESTION OF DEMOCRACY

What does all this mean as regards democracy? EU public documents regularly invoke democracy. The Laeken Declaration states, "The European Union derives its legitimacy from the democratic values it projects. . . . [T]he European project also derives its legitimacy from democratic, transparent and efficient institutions." Yet it also states, "The Union needs to become more democratic, more transparent and more efficient." In fact, the EU's "democratic deficit" has become a topic of extensive discussion. An entry under that heading in the *Encyclopedia of the European Union* begins, "In the mid-1990s it was generally accepted that the EU suffered from a democratic deficit."[6]

Diagnoses of the problem differ, but several common themes recur. First, the European Parliament, the only directly elected body in the EU, is extremely weak, bearing little of the power wielded by national parliaments. Yet national parliaments themselves are losing much of their influence on various matters now treated primarily at the EU level. Meanwhile, the EU organs that do exercise real power, especially the Council and the Commission, deliberate mostly in secret. Moreover, EU institutional structures and the process through which policies are made are exceedingly complex and difficult to grasp. Thus decision making within the

EU is frequently characterized as "opaque," "obscure," "unaccountable," and "remote" from its citizens. Sometimes added to these complaints is a broader concern about the lack of citizen identification with and attachment to the EU.

For those who remain committed to the idea of a federal European state, the way of remedying these deficits is simple: move toward a real parliament which would have the power to form the government of the EU. For Euroskeptics who want to roll back the power of the EU, the equally clearcut answer is that only returning power to national parliaments can eliminate the democracy deficit. Other intergovernmentalists, more favorably disposed toward the EU, tend to deny the seriousness of the problem. Noting that there has also been a trend within national governments to delegate more power to expert administrative bodies precisely in the areas of competence where the EU is most active, they suggest that the acquiescence of national parliaments to this tendency offers sufficient democratic legitimacy. But such arguments do little to assuage the discontent of European publics with the EU's opacity and remoteness. Hence the current efforts at reform, at simplification, and even at providing a real constitution for the European Union.

The question is whether and how this effort can succeed. If one believes that democracy is firmly tied to the framework of the state, it is difficult to see how a solution to the democratic deficit that is neither intergovernmentalist or fully federalist can be found. A successful effort to democratize the EU would inevitably push it in the direction of becoming a state. Today one might say that the EU enjoys a supremacy over its member states in moral and legal legitimacy, but the member states retain the supremacy in terms of democratic, and hence political, legitimacy (as well as real power and resources). If the EU were to gain full democratic legitimacy, the inevitable result would be the subordination of the member states.

For those who believe that the EU represents a new and unprecedented kind of polity, the problem takes on a different aspect. If democracy need not be tied to state structures, new possibilities for democratic innovation may emerge. Philippe C. Schmitter, for example, has emphasized "the growing dissociation between territorial constituencies and functional *compétences*" in the EU. He even conceives a future in which each European country could choose from "a menu of potential common tasks." Hence, "instead of a single Europe with recognized and contiguous boundaries . . . there would be multiple regional institutions [with different sets of members] acting autonomously to solve common problems and produce different public goods."[7] As Schmitter recognizes, however, it is not easy to imagine such a non-state arrangement remaining stable in the long run, nor to democratize it without devising radically new forms of citizenship, representation, and accountability.

Ultimately, the question of democracy and the European Union points to the larger question of the relation between democracy and the state. Perhaps the EU will indeed turn out to be the first postmodern polity, ushering in a new dispensation in which the traditional state is transcended and democracy assumes a novel shape. But if we are not entering a new political era of this kind, the prospects for a strong EU are probably not very bright. Old-fashioned federalists, as well as those who want an EU that is a world power in political and military as well as economic terms, constantly run up against the problem of trying to build a continental state in an intellectual and moral climate that is hostile to the predominance of the state. The policies successfully employed by European states in the past to forge a common culture, in part through universal conscription into a national army, would be anathema to the diversity-worshipping and antimilitary ethos of today's Europeans.

Despite the boredom it so often engenders, the EU is in many respects the most interesting and far-reaching political experiment of our time. Yet by combining extremely high political aspirations with an aversion to state-building, and in effect opting for a stateless or antipolitical politics, it may well condemn itself to continuing disappointment, perennial instability, and ultimate irrelevance.

8

Sovereignty and Democracy

2003

In July 2003, a "European Convention" chaired by former French President Valéry Giscard d'Estaing finished drafting a new constitution for the European Union, but the parallels with the Philadelphia Convention of 1787 that this inevitably conjures up for American observers are extremely misleading. Anyone who expects the debate over the EU constitution to mirror the historic contest in the United States between Federalists and Anti-Federalists is quickly disabused. That was an argument about the proper locus of sovereignty and the appropriate scale of the state. Politicians can sometimes be heard voicing such concerns in Europe today, but in scholarly and intellectual circles the predominant tendency is not to argue about where sovereignty should be lodged, but to call into question the concept of sovereignty; not to argue about how big the state should be, but to wonder about whether the era of the modern state is coming to an end.

This may seem odd at a time when the modern state seems to be enjoying the hour of its greatest triumph. Virtually the entire world now consists of independent states, their number greater than ever before. And the most important global institutions, beginning with the United Nations itself, are intergovernmental organizations whose members are states, represented by the delegates of their governments. Yet there is no denying the fact that in many quarters, especially in some of the advanced democracies, there is a widespread feeling that the modern state is becoming obsolete, that it is increasingly incapable of responding to the problems of the contemporary world and above all to the challenges posed by globalization. It is this feeling that shapes the moral and political context in which European unification is unfolding. In one sense, of course, the EU is merely a regional organization, but the debate over its future is intimately bound up with the issue of globalization.

Globalization is a subject on everyone's lips today, not just in Europe but around the world. I am inclined to believe that recent advances in telecommunications technology and in the internationalization of markets have created a greater degree of mutual interpenetration among societies worldwide than ever existed before. But the trends that are summed up by the term "globalization" are not new. Following the rise of multinational corporations and the oil price shocks of the 1970s, many observers called attention to the idea of international "interdependence." And some scholars have plausibly argued that there was greater international openness and mobility during the period prior to World War I than there is today. In my view, what is distinctive about the current discourse on globalization is the jaundiced view that it takes of the modern state. After having long been regarded as the culmination of political evolution and the indispensable framework for freedom and democracy, the state is now often seen as a historically contingent institution built on shaky moral foundations.

DECONSTRUCTING THE STATE

One scholar who appears to have been especially influential in shaping current thinking about the modern state is John Ruggie. Fittingly enough, Ruggie not only is a distinguished professor of international relations, but has recently served as assistant secretary-general of the United Nations. His writings, and especially his article "Territoriality and Beyond: Problematizing Modernity in International Relations," are widely cited not only in the academic literature but also in more policy-oriented discussions regarding the future of the European Union.[1] What Ruggie "problematizes" in his essay is not just modernity, but the modern state and the concept of sovereignty.

The discipline of international relations tends to take for granted the "modern system of states," Ruggie argues. Thus, while it is adept at understanding changes in the balance of power among states, it is poorly equipped to understand the more momentous kind of transformation that may result in "fundamental institutional discontinuity in the system of states." Yet there are signs that such a period of "epochal" change may now be upon us. This is seen both in the transformation of the global economy due to ever more extensive transnational links and in the rise of the European Union, which "may constitute nothing less than the emergence of the first postmodern international political form."

Ruggie's essay includes a brief account of the debate about postmodernism in the humanities, but for the purposes of international relations he distinguishes the modern from the postmodern in terms of their different "forms of configuring political space." The modern system of rule is based upon "territorially defined, fixed and mutually exclusive enclaves of legitimate domination. As such, it appears to be unique in human history." How else has political space been configured in the past? Ruggie refers briefly to primitive kin-based systems and to the conception of property rights held by nomadic peoples, but by far the greatest part of his analysis is devoted to the "nonexclusive territorial rule" that characterized medieval Europe, with its complex patterns of multiple allegiances and overlapping jurisdictions.

It is by analyzing the earlier transformation of the feudal order into the modern world of states claiming absolute and exclusive sovereignty over their territories that we can gain insight into the new transformation that may now be under way. The modern state has been invented or "socially constructed," and thus its persistence cannot be taken for granted. In fact, the European Union, where "the process of unbundling of territoriality has gone further than anywhere else," may point the way toward a postmodern future that will in important respects resemble the medieval past.

The general orientation of Ruggie's analysis is reflected in a great deal of contemporary writing about sovereignty, the nation-state, and the European Union. (To be sure, Ruggie draws upon a body of prior academic studies, most notably the work on the formation of the modern state prominently associated with Charles Tilly.[2]) One encounters in this literature surprisingly frequent references to the fleeting and historically contingent character of the modern nation-state. And the European Union is most often described not as the germ of some larger form of the nation-state (often disparagingly referred to as a "superstate"), but as a new kind of postmodern or "neomedieval" structure that transcends the "Westphalian" framework.

Yet while Ruggie's argument incorporates a number of useful insights, I believe that it is misguided in several crucial respects. The first is an overemphasis on the wholesale uniqueness of the modern state. It is true that the modern state differs in some ways from all previous political orders, and its persistence, despite its current worldwide predominance, should not simply be taken for granted. Yet the fact that the modern state is new is sometimes elided into the view that the division of the world into separate political orders is also something new. Ruggie's assertion that an order based upon "territorially defined, fixed and mutually exclusive enclaves of legitimate domination . . . appears to be unique in human history" is, I believe, simply wrong.

Analyses like Ruggie's that hold that the modern state was invented or constructed tend to take the feudal Europe that preceded it as a more gradually evolved and thus somehow more natural and less arbitrary form of political order. They do not consider the possibility that the feudal order, shaped by the universalist claims of pope and emperor, was itself a radical departure in human history, occasioned by the rise of Christian revelation. But this is surely how feudalism was viewed by the theoretical founders of modern politics.

The notion that the earlier transition from feudalism to modernity somehow supplies the key to understanding the coming transformation to a new system that will transcend modernity recalls the doctrine of Karl Marx. And as is also true of the Marxist schema, Ruggie's perspective has very great difficulty fitting the ancient world into its analytical framework. Most such contemporary approaches, including Ruggie's, do not even try to account for classical Greece and Rome; they simply ignore them. Willful neglect of the ancient city is, in fact, a striking feature of this entire literature. One can read histories of the state or of international state systems that deal with primitive tribes, nomadic peoples, the Chinese Empire, ancient India, and the Islamic world but do not even have an entry in the index for ancient Greece. This is especially odd, first, because the cities of ancient Greece certainly constituted a system of political units based on "territorially defined, fixed and mutually exclusive enclaves of legitimate domination" and, second, because part of the inspiration for the creation of the modern European state unmistakably came from the rediscovery of ancient political thought and practice.

After all, even medieval political thought was decisively shaped by the recovery of the works of Aristotle. It is true that early modern thinkers like Machiavelli and Hobbes openly attacked classical political thought and sought to create or to justify a political order that would differ in crucial respects from the ancient city; yet a major aim of these founders of modern political philosophy was to recover the autonomy and supremacy of political life that had characterized classical Greece and Rome. Machiavelli's most comprehensive work consists of discourses on Livy's history of Rome, and Hobbes's earliest published writing was a translation of Thucydides's history of the Peloponnesian war. Moreover, the peculiarly modern doctrine of sovereignty first developed by Bodin and Hobbes, however it may differ in other ways from the classical understanding, agrees with the Aristotelian view that the political order is the highest association or the supreme community—at least in the sense of not being properly subject to any external power.

The focus on the medieval world and neglect of the ancient in the literature to which Ruggie's essay belongs tend to be paralleled by a lack of concern with the issue of self-government or democracy. Those who write approvingly of the Holy Roman Empire as a model for Europe[3] or praise the diversity and permeability of borders in the "pre-Westphalian" era do not appear to reflect on the human consequences of those arrangements. It is not mere happenstance that the feudal period was a time not only of disorder but of oppression and severe inequality. An absence of firm borders and of clear lines of jurisdiction may not be a problem in empires or other political forms where governments are not accountable to their citizens. But if the citizens are to govern, or at least to hold their governors accountable, it must be clear who is and who is not included in the polity. And it is hard to see how this can be accomplished without clear lines of demarcation indicating whose voices have the right to be counted.

There is more than a merely verbal connection between the modern concept of sovereignty and the contemporary idea of the sovereignty of the people. Notwithstanding the fact that Bodin and Hobbes were champions of monarchy, it is their doctrine of sovereignty that prepared the way for the notion that all political power ultimately derives from the consent of naturally free and equal individuals. It is the modern nation-state that provided the indispensable framework for building a political order that protects the rights and heeds the voices of all the people who belong to it.[4]

Two of the leading contemporary scholars of democracy, Juan Linz and Alfred Stepan, affirm the necessity of this link with particular forcefulness: "[W]ithout a state," they argue, "no modern democracy is possible. . . . Modern democratic government is inevitably linked to stateness. Without a state, there can be no citizenship; without citizenship, there can be no democracy."[5]

DEMOCRACY WITHOUT SOVEREIGNTY?

What, then, is the attitude toward democracy of those who proclaim the obsolescence of the nation-state and welcome the erosion of the "Westphalian" notion of sovereignty? While there are some who ignore or are indifferent to this question, it would be inaccurate and unfair to claim that this is the general view of the champions of transnationalism. There is, for example, a lively and intense debate about the EU's "democracy deficit" or "legitimacy deficit" and how to repair it. This concern even appears prominently in the EU's Laeken Declaration, the official document that initiated the process leading to the new draft constitution. A cynic might say that this is the defensive response of European elites, worried that disillusionment among European publics with the remote and opaque decision making of the EU may derail the entire project of "ever closer union." But I believe that it also reflects the fact that the global prestige of the democratic principle is perhaps higher than it has ever been—notwithstanding the growing tendency to question the legitimacy of the modern state.

As a result, many students and proponents of the EU seem to be groping toward the view that the EU can become a democratic *non*-state. They refuse to accept the dichotomy according to which the EU must be *either* (1) an essentially intergovernmental organization that derives its democratic legitimacy through the national parliaments of its member states *or* (2) a genuine federal state that derives its democratic legitimacy through governing institutions directly responsible to the European electorate. They say, with more than a little justification, that the EU already has gone well beyond being a merely intergovernmental institution yet falls far short of being a federal state. At the same time, their argument is not that the EU has found some "middle way" between intergovernmentalism and traditional federalism but rather that its organizing principles must be understood as existing on a different plane from the continuum that runs from intergovernmentalism to federalism. Thus, they define the EU as a non-state, non-nation polity (or entity).[6]

It may be true that so far this is largely the language of academics rather than politicians or publics, but the argument has a considerable attraction for the latter as well. First, this non-state conception appeals to a strong antipolitical disposition that is seen today in many parts of the world but is especially powerful in Europe. This disposition is reflected in the enormous prestige enjoyed by "civil society" and by "nongovernmental organizations," as compared to political parties or to governments. One way of viewing the non-state vision of the EU is that it promises to provide governance *without* the need for government. Indeed, some Europeans, far from wishing to build a new kind of polity, seem to aspire to the creation of a new *non*governmental organization—the EU as the world's largest and most influential NGO. Second, the non-state conception seems to offer a means of what is frequently referred to as "squaring the circle"—that is, building an ever closer European Union without taking away the sovereignty of member states that many Europeans continue to hold dear.

According to the classic modern doctrine of sovereignty, of course, it was regarded as impossible to maintain sovereignty in both a political union and its constituent parts. In contemporary language, one might say that the lodging of sovereignty was regarded as a kind of "zero-sum game." Here is how Alexander Hamilton, in *Federalist* 15, characterizes the opponents of the Constitution drafted by the Philadelphia Convention: They aim, he charges, "at things repugnant and irreconcilable; at an augmentation of federal authority without a diminution of State authority; at sovereignty in the Union and complete independence in the members. They still, in fine, seem to cherish with blind devotion the political monster of an *imperium in imperio*."[7]

A bit further on, Hamilton elaborates on what he calls "the characteristic difference between a league and a government"—namely, that only the latter can extend its authority to individuals, while the authority of the former reaches no further than to member governments. Government, according to Hamilton, involves the power not only of making laws, but of enforcing them. For if they are without sanctions, "resolutions or commands which pretend to be laws will, in fact, amount to nothing more than advice or recommendation." While governments may deal with recalcitrant individuals through the "courts and ministers of justice," there is no way a league can enforce its decisions against one of the sovereign entities that compose it without resorting to military force. Thus, in a league "every breach of the laws must involve a state of war; and military execution must become the only instrument of civil obedience."

The *Federalist* goes on to support this reasoning by appeals both to the nature of man and to the experience of previous confederations. Because men love power, those who exercise sovereignty are likely to resist attempts to constrain or direct them. Thus, in confederations that attempt to unite sovereign bodies, there is inevitably a centrifugal tendency for the parts to free themselves from the center. The subsequent numbers of the *Federalist* then explore the experience of confederations both ancient and modern. The conclusion drawn from this examination of the historical record is emphatically stated at the end of *Federalist* 20 (a paper sometimes attributed jointly to Hamilton and James Madison)—namely, "that a sovereignty over sovereigns, a government over governments, a legislation for communities, as contradistinguished from individuals, as it is a solecism in theory, so in practice it is subversive of the order and ends of civil polity, by substituting *violence* in place of the mild and salutary coercion of the magistracy."

Hamilton justifies this sweeping conclusion by appealing to "experience [which] is the oracle of truth." Yet proponents of the new views put forward by theorists of the European Union would point precisely to the experience of European integration to contradict Hamilton's conclusions. First of all, though in many respects it seems closer to a league than to a government in Hamilton's terms, the EU, thanks to various rulings of the European Court and their acceptance by national courts, does have authority that in important respects reaches to individuals as well as collectivities. Second, in spite of the lack of a mechanism to enforce compliance, the decisions of the EU are largely accepted by member states—and this without resort to the sword.

In fact, the EU seems to present the spectacle of constituent units obeying the dictates of the center not only without violence but even without visible coercion. In trying to understand this unprecedented phenomenon, I have found particularly helpful a formulation offered by J. H. H. Weiler, one of the most distinguished scholars of European law. Weiler argues that the EU has evolved a federal constitutional or *legal* structure alongside a largely "confederal" or intergovernmental *political* structure.[8] In other words, Europe has accepted the "constitutional discipline" characteristic of federalism without becoming a federal state. In effect, it has become a federal non-state whose decisions are accepted voluntarily by its constituent units rather than backed up by the modes of hierarchical coercion classically employed by the modern state. In fact, the EU combines a "top-to-bottom hierarchy of norms" with "a bottom-to-top hierarchy of . . . real power." It achieves what Hamilton would have regarded as either disastrous or impossible—the separation of law from the power to enforce it.

However accurate Weiler's analysis may be in describing the current state of the EU, it surely raises a couple of larger questions: First, what conditions have enabled this structure to work so far, and can it continue to do so? Second, presuming that the federal non-state can continue to maintain itself, what would be the ultimate consequences for democracy? The first of these questions concerns the viability or practicability of the federal non-state, while the second concerns its ultimate desirability. I cannot hope to address these matters in more than a preliminary way here, but let me try to offer a few reflections about them.

WAR AND THE POSTMODERN STATE

In seeking to understand what has enabled the EU to function effectively as a federal non-state, I would emphasize the fact that its member states are all liberal democracies. This means not only that they are "open societies" but that they are averse to using force against other open societies. Here I think that what has been dubbed the "democratic peace" thesis is directly relevant. That thesis, based on an imposing record of historical evidence, holds that liberal democracies rarely if ever fight wars against each other (though they are quite prone to fight wars against countries that are not liberal democracies). The web of ties that bind member states of the EU has undoubtedly contributed to the sense that war among them is unthinkable, but one might argue that the nature of the member states is more important in this regard than the framework that connects them. After all, war is equally unthinkable between an EU member state and a nonmember like Norway or Switzerland, just as it is unthinkable between the United States and Canada or between Australia and New Zealand.

The fact that contemporary liberal democracies do not fear that force will be used against them by their fellow liberal democracies makes possible a previously unprecedented degree of integration among them. In Europe, a region where most regimes—and certainly the most powerful ones—are liberal democracies, it has made possible the success of the European Union in achieving an extraordinary degree of cooperation without erecting a "superstate." In understanding this achievement I have found very useful the analysis offered by the British diplomat Robert Cooper (a former foreign policy advisor to Prime Minister Tony Blair who is now working as director-general for external and politico-military affairs for the Council of the European Union). In his remarkably concise essay *The Postmodern State and the World Order*, Cooper provides what, to my mind, is a much more persuasive case than does John Ruggie for the novelty of the EU and for the willingness of its member states to surrender some of their sovereignty.[9]

Cooper convincingly demonstrates that there has been a fundamental change in the international aims and behavior of many of the advanced democracies, but he also emphasizes that the postmodern order most clearly represented by the EU constitutes only one portion of today's world. For it coexists with two other orders: the modern order of robust national states still jealous of their sovereignty (among his examples are India, China, and Saddam Hussein's Iraq) and the premodern order of "failed states" (Afghanistan, Somalia, Sierra Leone) incapable of exercising real control over their territories. This means that the postmodern states, while they may eschew the use of force among themselves, cannot wholly escape the need of employing it in their dealings with modern and premodern states. It also means that the ability to preserve and enhance the postmodern achievements of the EU depends on a willingness to depart from the norms of postmodern behavior and to employ the "rougher methods of an earlier era" when the situation demands. As Cooper puts it, "Among ourselves, we keep the law but when we are operating in the jungle, we must also use the laws of the jungle."

As we have recently witnessed, however, the perceived need to resort to "rougher methods," especially those involving the use of military force, tends to create political disputes among postmodern states that are not easily resolved consensually. Some would no doubt argue that the current contentions within the EU are largely provoked by the policies of the United States and that the fault lines dividing Europeans have their origins in Washington. Others would surely respond that the U.S. security umbrella provides the indispensable shelter that allows the EU to function as a wholly civilian non-state polity.

Be that as it may, the difficulty underlined by Cooper remains. Even if the European Union succeeds in taming national sovereignty and in subordinating force to law within its own postmodern sphere, can it continue to resist the pressures and dangers that arise from the still untamed parts of the world? As Cooper notes, "States reared on *raison d'état* and power politics make uncomfortable neighbors for the postmodern democratic conscience. Supposing the world develops . . . into an intercontinental struggle. Would Europe be equipped for that?" To put it somewhat differently, will a nonstate be able to defend and preserve itself in a world that still contains powerful modern states? Or would such external pressure drive Europeans to try to recover their "stateness," whether by the formation of a real European "superstate" or by a reassertion of sovereignty at the level of the nation-state?[10]

So even if Europe is undergoing a far-reaching transformation such that the old notions of sovereignty no longer apply within the intra-European sphere, the question remains whether "postmodernism in one region" can really work. Can Europe renounce the use of force if other parts of the world refuse to do so? And can Europe continue to govern itself within a non-state framework if its member states must continually wrestle with life-and-death issues of war and peace that intrude upon it from other regions? The EU's perennial difficulties in fashioning a common foreign policy underline the seriousness of this dilemma.

TRANSCENDING THE STATE?

But let us for argument's sake presume that the rest of the world can be postmodernized and, thus, that this problem can be resolved. There would still remain the question of what might be lost in leaving behind or transcending the nation-state. Here I have in mind precisely the issue of democracy. This problem is also briefly noted by Cooper, who formulates it in the following terms: "A difficulty for the postmodern state . . . is that democracy and democratic institutions are firmly wedded to the territorial state. . . . Economy, law-making, and defense may be increasingly embedded in international frameworks, and the borders of territory may be less important, but identity and democratic institutions remain primarily national."

Cooper's reference here to identity being "primarily national" raises an important ambiguity inherent in the word "national," so let me make clear that I am not suggesting that political identity must be tied to some form of ethnicity. As the case of the United States proves, such identity can be established among citizens of very diverse ethnic origins. Though it would not be easy, I do not think it is out of the question that a European political identity could be nurtured that would come to supersede the attachment of Europeans to their existing national states. So I am not arguing that European unification as such is hostile to democracy, or that the only way to preserve democracy in Europe is to reaffirm the sovereignty of the EU's member states. I am not a "Euroskeptic."

My argument is that for democracy to work, there must be an overarching political order to which people feel they owe their primary political loyalty—in short, a state, with clear boundaries and clear distinctions as to who does and does not enjoy the rights and obligations of citizenship. In principle, such an order could equally well be constituted at the level of the European Union or remain at the level of its member states. What I doubt is that it is possible to square the circle of competing sovereignties over the long run or that democracy can work outside or across the framework of a sovereign state. So my plea is that those who are seriously devoted to democracy reconsider their devaluation of the state, or at least think harder about how it can be left behind without also undermining democracy.

The strong tendency today for many proponents of liberal democracy to turn against the state, despite the long and intimate relationship between liberal democracy and the modern state, is striking. I think the reason behind it lies not only in certain historical developments but in a tension that has always existed at the heart of liberal democracy. In earlier chapters I have explored the tension between the liberal and the democratic elements that form the cohesive but unstable compound known as liberal democracy. The liberal or cosmopolitan element, which emphasizes the universal human rights of the individual, fits uneasily with the particularistic demands of self-government and citizenship that constitute its specifically democratic element. In my view, the European Union, especially as understood by the approach that I have been discussing, represents the exaltation of liberal democracy's liberal aspect at the expense of its democratic aspect. The real issue is whether liberalism can flourish—or even survive—if it is not anchored in the framework of a democratic state. Can liberalism, as it were, outgrow the state and sustain itself within a transnational or cosmopolitan order?

The most perceptive account of the historical and philosophical dialectic involving democracy and the nation-state has been presented by the French political philosopher Pierre Manent. As he puts it, "One might say that the democratic principle, after having used the nation as an instrument or vehicle, abandons it by the wayside. This would not be worrisome if a new vehicle were available or clearly under construction. This new *political* form, however, is nowhere in sight."[11] I emphasize the word *political* because Manent is of course aware that many see the European Union as just such a vehicle. His contention, however, is that "Europe refuses to define itself politically," preferring to see itself in cultural or civilizational terms—or, at any rate, refusing to constitute itself as a state.

Why, according to Manent, does the democratic principle (which holds that human beings are by nature free and equal and that all political legitimacy must be rooted in their consent) abandon or even turn against the state? He links this development to the fact that the boundaries or limits of the particular political unit embodied in the state cannot themselves be justified democratically. All existing states owe their boundaries to historical contingencies—especially to the outcome of wars—that are wholly arbitrary from a strictly democratic perspective. The democratic principle of popular sovereignty or self-determination fails to provide any basis for deciding how to define the people that is sovereign or the collective self that is to determine its own fate. Thus, the distinction between the citizen and the outsider can appear ultimately arbitrary and even unjust. From a cosmopolitan perspective it seems to be one more example of "discrimination," or of using an artificial distinction to justify treating some people differently from others.

Thus, the democratic principle of human freedom and equality can be turned against the state in the name of the individual and of the common humanity that he shares with citizens and noncitizens alike. Once the democratic principle is pushed to the point where it breaks down the framework of the nation-state, Manent argues, it in effect turns against political life as such. That is, it calls into question the possibility of any self-governing community.

Political life requires that the political community be sovereign, that it establish the laws under which other human associations or communities operate. It is the public sphere that ultimately determines the boundaries of the private sphere, however capacious those boundaries may be. And the public sphere can exist only if people become fellow citizens, if they agree to be governed by the decisions made through a legitimate political process, even when these decisions may require that they part with their property or risk their lives. As Manent emphasizes, to have a political order people must be willing to "put things in common," to become part of a community that in important respects must set itself off from those who are not members. Only in that way can it govern itself.

CITIZENS AND THE OTHER

The most revealing account that I have found of the principled and moral refusal to "put things in common" in a political fashion is provided by J. H. H. Weiler in the essay cited above. Not coincidentally, that essay concludes by explicitly casting doubt on the value of democracy. For Weiler, Europe's non-state constitutional federalism "represents . . . its deepest set of values," rooted in what he calls the Principle of Constitutional Tolerance. This principle rejects not just nationalism but even the idea of "constitutional patriotism," of an ethos that "implicitly celebrates a supposed unique moral identity, the wisdom, and yes, the superiority of the authors of the constitution, the people, the constitutional *demos.*" Weiler denies that democracy should be regarded as a goal of the EU. The goal, instead, "is to try, and try again, to live a life of decency, to honour our creation in the image of God, or the secular equivalent." And "in the realm of the social, in the public square, the relationship to the alien is at the core of such decency." Nothing is "normatively more important to the human condition and to our multicultural societies."

How, then, should we deal with the alien? Weiler describes two strategies. The first, which involves inviting the alien to become one of us, for example, by making him a fellow citizen, is rejected because "it risks robbing him of his identity." It is thus "a form of dangerous internal and external intolerance." Instead, Weiler argues in favor of a strategy that maintains boundaries and respects difference, but in which "one is commanded to reach over the boundary and accept [the alien], in his alienship, as oneself." This points to the "deeper spiritual meaning" of Europe's non-statist constitutional architecture. It calls upon Europeans to bond not with fellow citizens but precisely with *others*. It asks them to "compromise" their "self-determination" in the name of tolerance. It calls for voluntary subordination to the decisions of others, "which constitutes an act of true liberty and emancipation from collective self-arrogance and constitutional fetishism." In sum, Weiler attacks the moral basis of the constitutional democratic state, in which people become fellow citizens by "putting things in common," in favor of the allegedly more elevated principle of respecting what is alien.

Weiler's essay is one of the most brilliant things I have read about the European Union, but, as is no doubt apparent, I believe it is profoundly misguided, both morally and practically. Central to Weiler's discussion is his invocation of the fact that "Europe was built on the ashes of World War II, which witnessed the most horrific alienation of those thought of as aliens; an alienation which became annihilation." But what is the proper lesson to be drawn from the Holocaust? Is it that the constitutional democratic state is inadequate, or is it that the worst evils come from the failure to establish and consolidate constitutional democratic states? To me, it seems obvious that the correct lesson is the latter. Certainly, I know that if neo-Nazis or other alien-haters were to target me, I would vastly prefer to entrust my rights and my fate to the protections offered by a constitutional democratic state that combines law with force than to a transnational architecture of any sort.

9

Two Kinds of Internationalism

2005

It is often said that a prime cause of the dissension between the United States and Europe is the differing views about international cooperation that prevail on opposite sides of the Atlantic: Europeans, shaped by their experience with EU integration, are devoted to multilateralism, while Americans exhibit an increasing penchant for unilateralism. And there is no question that on a number of high-profile issues in recent years the United States has taken stands that have put it in opposition not only to Europe but to what is often referred to as "the international community." This includes the war in Iraq (though on this matter Europe itself was very much divided), as well as such issues as the Kyoto Protocol on global warming, and the creation of the International Criminal Court. The United States not only has been willing to oppose such international agreements, but has been much more concerned than European nations with defending the principle of national sovereignty and much more ready to question the moral supremacy of the United Nations or of international opinion.

Yet there is a paradox here. For at the same time, the United States is widely viewed as the prime agent of "globalization" and the homogenization that it brings in its wake. Thus the anti-globalization movement, which is animated in part by the desire to preserve distinctive national and cultural traditions and ways of life, is a hotbed of anti-Americanism. The United States is charged with being the most universalist of countries, with seeking to impose Western-style democracy on peoples for whom it is inappropriate, with believing that the whole world is—or at least can or should be—like America.

Moreover, throughout the twentieth century, the United States was a leader in building the institutions that came to symbolize liberal internationalism.

It was President Woodrow Wilson who was the guiding spirit behind the formation of the League of Nations and President Franklin Roosevelt who was the guiding spirit behind the creation of the United Nations. It is also true, of course, that the U.S. Senate, reflecting the isolationist strands in American political culture, rejected American membership in the League. After the Second World War, however, the United States largely overcame its older isolationist tendencies and became the key architect of the ensemble of multilateral institutions that still shape the international landscape.

What accounts, then, for the opposition to multilateralism that is seen as guiding U.S. policy in the new century? Has there been a dramatic change in the U.S. outlook and its approach to international affairs, prompted perhaps by its emergence as the world's only superpower or by the trauma of 9/11? Or has the real change been in the way the concept of multilateralism has come to be understood today, so that U.S. policy, despite a fundamental continuity, now appears to be out of sync with world opinion? In other words, might it be that the United States is hostile to a new version of multilateralism, while largely remaining faithful to the old? Of course, these two explanations need not be mutually exclusive. There probably has been a certain alteration in the expression, if not the substance, of American policy, but I believe that a more fundamental shift has occurred in the nature and meaning of multilateralism.

This shift has been hailed by the champions of a remodeled multilateralism, who stress the distinction between the old "liberal internationalism" and the new "globalism." The former refers to the vision that is reflected in the UN Charter—and indeed in the very name of the United Nations. This is the concept of a league or organization of states whose purposes (to quote from the UN Charter) are to "maintain international peace and security," "develop friendly relations among nations," "achieve international cooperation" in economic, social, and cultural matters and in promoting human rights, and "be a centre for harmonizing the actions of nations in the attainment of these common ends." The UN was understood primarily as an organization of sovereign states, represented by their governments. The very first principle enunciated in the Charter states: "The Organization is based on the principle of the sovereign equality of its Members." But this brand of multilateralism today is regarded as in many respects outmoded, if not retrograde. In the words of former UN assistant secretary-general John Ruggie, "Simply put, postwar institutions, including the United Nations, were built for an inter-*national* world, but we have entered a *global* world. International institutions were designed to reduce *external* frictions between states; our challenge today is to devise more *inclusive* forms of global governance."[1]

What exactly is the nature of the new globalism toward which Ruggie and thinkers like him point? This is not so easy to pin down, though the underlying premises of the "globalists" are quite clear: Thanks to technological advances, especially in communications, the world is more interconnected than ever before. Instead of separate national industries and economies, today we have multinational companies and integrated global markets. At the same time, threats as well as opportunities have gone global. Drug traffickers and other criminal networks operate across borders, and of course environmental dangers like global warming and health dangers like AIDS cannot be confined within national boundaries. Meanwhile, the greatest dangers to peace no longer seem to arise from traditional sorts of interstate hostility, but from non-state terrorist organizations and from internecine conflict within states. So the challenges confronting us are increasingly global, while our political institutions remain essentially national and hence unable to cope with this new wave of problems.

Thus the agenda of the new multilateralism is to close the "global governance gaps" that result from the mismatch between the global scale of contemporary problems and the merely national reach of the most effective political institutions. Since it is obviously beyond our power to shrink the scale of the problems, the favored solution is to globalize our political institutions. Yet for a variety of both practical and theoretical reasons, the "globalists" do not advocate a world state or even world federalism. Instead, they seem to favor mechanisms of global governance that involve "networks" of international organizations, national governments, the private sector, labor unions, and NGOs. They propose not to abolish existing national states, but to reduce them to one player among many—and one with a weaker claim to moral legitimacy than international organizations or "global civil society." Nor do they seem to worry very much about the lack of democratic accountability that will inevitably beset these new mechanisms of global governance.

This is not the place to engage in a detailed analysis of the new multilateralism, which is reflected in such initiatives as the Kyoto Protocol and the International Criminal Court. The point I want to emphasize here is that multilateralism is a term that can cover a wide range of practices and approaches, and that current versions of it are much more expansive than was traditional "liberal internationalism." Perhaps a similar example from recent history can help make this point clearer. The isolation of the United States in international organizations is hardly a new phenomenon. The United States was often on the losing side of lopsided votes in the UN General Assembly back in the 1970s and 1980s. That was the period when the G-77, the group of developing nations at the UN, was pressing for a New International Economic Order. This involved a range of measures calling for redistribution from richer to poorer nations and for greater regulation of international business. Among the initiatives on which the United States was isolated in opposition in those days was something called "Global

Negotiations," which was meant to restructure the world economy under the aegis of the UN General Assembly.

Whatever the merits of the U.S. position on these issues, it would be misleading to ascribe it to hostility to multilateralism as such rather than to concerns about the proper scope and locus of multinational authority. In fact, American opposition to Global Negotiations was based in part on the grounds that they would infringe upon the autonomy of the specialized international agencies dealing with economic issues, especially the International Monetary Fund, another U.S.-inspired creation of the postwar era. There were then, and remain today, all kinds of multilateral activities that the United States regards as vital. Americans are not unilateralists. They believe, however, that international cooperation should adhere to limits that respect national sovereignty. Put somewhat differently, Americans believe in universal principles, but hold that their implementation should be the business of democratically elected and accountable national governments.[2]

THE DECLARATION OF INDEPENDENCE

This outlook, which I believe has heretofore characterized modern liberal democracy as such, is deeply rooted in American history and experience. If we turn to America's founding political document, the Declaration of Independence, we find a striking juxtaposition of an invocation of universal principles and an insistence on the right of a particular people to determine its own destiny. In declaring their independence from the British Crown, the representatives of the American colonies affirmed their right to a "separate and equal station" among the "Powers of the Earth" and to do all the "Acts and Things which Independent States may of right do." This includes, of course, the right to make war, and the Declaration notes that the former colonies hold the British, "as we hold the rest of Mankind, Enemies in War, in Peace, Friends."

Yet, although the bulk of the document enumerates the specific transgressions of the Crown that the colonists cite to justify their rebellion, the Declaration's best-known passage asserts the most universal of principles:

> We hold these truths to be self-evident, that all Men are created equal, that they are endowed by their Creator with certain unalienable Rights, that among these are Life, Liberty and the pursuit of Happiness.—That to secure these rights, Governments are instituted among Men, deriving their just powers from the consent of the governed,—That whenever any Form of Government becomes destructive of these ends, it is the Right of the People to alter or to abolish it, and to institute new Government, laying its foundations on such principles, and organizing its powers in such form, as to them shall seem most likely to effect their Safety and Happiness.

The contrast between the universalist and particularistic aspects of the Declaration was dramatically underlined by Abraham Lincoln in paying tribute to its principal author, Thomas Jefferson: "All honor to Jefferson," Lincoln wrote, "to the man who, in the concrete pressure of a struggle for national independence by a single people, had the coolness, forecast, and capacity to introduce into a merely revolutionary document, an abstract truth, applicable to all men and all times, and so to embalm it there, that to-day, and in all coming days, it shall be a rebuke and a stumbling-block to the very harbingers of re-appearing tyranny and oppression."[3] Yet, as is indicated by the latter part of the passage from the Declaration cited above, these abstract or self-evident truths were an essential part of the justification for the revolution: The proper goal of government is to secure the rights of individuals; government derives its legitimacy from the consent of the governed; and the people have the right to alter or abolish their government when it no longer secures their rights or retains their consent. The rights of man are the same everywhere, but each people may decide for itself how best to secure them, when to bestow its consent upon government, and when to withdraw that consent and to seek a new government.

LOCKEAN PRINCIPLES

As has often been observed, the doctrine of the Declaration of Independence is largely derived from John Locke's *Second Treatise of Government,* and I believe that an analysis of that work can help us to understand the peculiar combination of universalism and particularism that characterizes liberal democracy. It also may illuminate the way Americans still tend to think about foreign policy. At the very outset of his now famous article "Power and Weakness," Robert Kagan describes contemporary transatlantic divergences in terms of Europeans entering a Kantian "paradise of peace and prosperity," while the United States remains mired in an "anarchic Hobbesian world."[4] Such shorthand descriptions are always crude exaggerations, of course, but they also have their uses. Only I would say that Kagan would have been more accurate to characterize the United States as Lockean rather than Hobbesian. For the American understanding of the principles of both domestic governance and foreign relations is much closer to that of Locke than to that of Hobbes.

The distinction I would draw between Locke and Hobbes is rather different from some common interpretations of these two thinkers. Sociologist Amitai Etzioni, for example, in his *From Empire to Community,* has a chapter entitled "Hobbesian versus Lockean Global Agendas."[5] Etzioni contrasts Hobbes's realistic concern with protecting the security of citizens, by force if necessary, with Locke's more idealistic concern with liberty and rights. I believe that this is a faulty of reading Locke, whose emphasis on security is no less intense than Hobbes's, but who disagrees about how security can best be obtained (not, he insists, by submitting to the authority of an absolute ruler). Moreover, Locke is more martial in spirit and in some respects more ready to endorse the use of force than Hobbes had been.

Like the Declaration of Independence, Locke's *Second Treatise* begins with the universal, examining the natural condition of mankind prior to or apart from any political community. By considering what he calls (following Hobbes) the "state of nature," Locke deduces the "equal right, that every man hath, to his natural freedom, without being subjected to the will or authority of any other man."[6] Since there is no natural basis for the rule of some men over others, Locke plausibly concludes that such rule can be legitimate only if it derives from the *consent* of the individuals who live under it. Although he does not deny that some human beings may excel in virtue or merit, Locke insists that such superiority does not give them any just title to rule others. Men are naturally equal in the decisive respect—they all have the right to do what they think is needful for their own self-preservation without having to seek the permission of anyone else.

The state of nature, Locke asserts, "has a law of nature to govern it." That law of nature, whose metaphysical and moral status is the subject of great controversy among students of Locke, instructs everyone that, "when his own preservation comes not in competition," he ought to do "as much as he can, to preserve the rest of mankind." It similarly teaches him that he may not harm others "unless it be to do justice on an offender" against that law. Under the law of nature, human beings all share in "one community of nature," a community coextensive with the species as a whole. In the state of nature, the community of men is no less universal than are their rights.[7]

Why, then, should human beings ever leave the universal freedom and community found in the state of nature? Locke himself poses this question very explicitly: "If man in the state of nature be so free, as has been said; if he be absolute lord of his own person and possessions, equal to the greatest, and subject to no body, why will he part with his freedom? Why will he give up this empire and subject himself to the dominion and control of any other power?" Locke's answer is that "though in the state of nature he hath such a right, yet the enjoyment of it is very uncertain, and constantly exposed to the invasion of others: for all being kings as much as he, every man his equal, and the greater part no strict observers of equity and justice, the enjoyment of the property he has in this state is very unsafe, very unsecure." Because of the uncertainties involved in establishing the precise commands of the law of nature and the difficulties in achieving its impartial and effective enforcement, mankind in the state of nature is in an "ill condition," one characterized by many "defects" and "inconveniences" and "full of fears and continual dangers." So for the sake of their safety and security, people are willing to give up their absolute freedom and a portion of their natural rights by agreeing with others to join what Locke calls political society. Such a society must supply three key elements that are "wanting" in the state of nature: "an established, settled, known law" that is accepted by everyone; impartial judges with authority to make decisions on the basis of that law; and a power that can give these decisions "due execution."[8]

In contrast with the state of nature, the political communities that men form are not universal but partial societies, even though their goal is protecting the universal rights of their members. Locke draws this distinction between the universal and the particular quite explicitly. In the state of nature, he says, all mankind "are one community, make up one society, distinct from all other creatures." It is only the fact that men cannot be relied upon to obey the law of nature that creates the "necessity that men should separate from this great and natural community, and by positive agreements combine into smaller and *divided* associations" (italics mine). A man must give up certain of his natural rights or "powers" when "he joins in a *private*, if I may so call it, or *particular* politic society and incorporates into any commonwealth separate from the rest of mankind" (italics mine).[9]

The power "of doing whatsoever he thought fit for the preservation of himself and *the rest of mankind*, he gives up to be regulated by laws made by the society, so far forth as the preservation of himself, and *the rest of that society* shall require" (italics mine). He also wholly gives up to the society his power of punishing violations of the law of nature. By joining a commonwealth, men exchange their natural but unreliably enforced obligation to preserve all their fellow human beings for a specific and strictly enforced obligation to preserve the other members of their own particular society. To fulfill the latter obligation, they may even be required to sacrifice their own preservation, as in the case of martial discipline, which "requires an absolute obedience to the command of every superior officer, and it is justly death to disobey or dispute the most dangerous or unreasonable of them."[10]

The command of natural law to preserve all of mankind thus comes to be outweighed by the command of positive law to defend the community to which one belongs. More generally, a universal law whose provisions are unclear and whose enforcement is uncertain gives way before a set of particular or positive laws that are clearly promulgated and reliably enforced. The source of those positive laws is the legislature, "the supreme power of the commonwealth," which should be "chosen and appointed" by the people and thus is backed by the people's consent and authority. "And therefore," Locke concludes, "all the obedience, which by the most solemn ties any one can be obliged to pay, ultimately terminates in this supreme power and is directed by those laws which it enacts." Correspondingly, the obligation of the people's rulers or representatives is not to benefit mankind at large but to serve the public good of the particular society that they govern. And it is to the members of that society that they are accountable.[11]

CONSTITUTING POLITICAL SOCIETIES

All this raises the question of how the boundaries of political societies or the composition and extent of their membership are to be established. Although Locke does not offer a systematic treatment of this question, it is addressed at various points within the *Second Treatise*, but from two different perspectives. Sometimes he discusses the ways in which societies actually developed historically, and at other times he focuses on the question of legitimacy—and it must be noted that not infrequently he seems intentionally to blur this distinction. Locke's historical speculations cover both societies formed peacefully on the basis of familial ties (in which political power was first entrusted to the father) and societies carved out by the conqueror's sword. Yet Locke emphatically insists that neither paternity nor conquest can give a *right* to political power. Such a right can come only from the consent of those who are to be governed.

Beyond the principle of consent, Locke does not offer any standard for determining who should belong to the commonwealth. He has very little to say about nationality in the sense of ethnicity. In the chapter "Of Conquest," he disputes the claim that "the English monarchy is founded in the Norman conquest," noting that English laws make no distinction between descendants of the conquered Saxons and Britons and descendants of the Normans who fought with the conqueror. And he adds that it "seldom happens, that the conquerors and conquered never incorporate into one people under the same laws and freedom." Yet later in this same chapter he argues that the descendants of a conquered people who were forced to submit to the government of a conqueror have a right to cast off the yoke imposed on their ancestors: "Who doubts but the Grecian christians, descendants of the ancient possessors of that country, may justly cast off the Turkish yoke, which they have so long groaned under, whenever they have an opportunity to do it?" The difference between the two cases appears to come down to the fact that the Grecian Christians, having maintained their feeling of separateness and never having agreed (or been allowed) to incorporate into one people with the Turks, have never really consented to the government under which they live. Membership in a legitimately governed commonwealth, then, is determined only by consent, though people's willingness to bestow their consent may indeed be affected by considerations of nationality or ethnicity.[12]

In his treatment of conquest, Locke clearly diverges from Hobbes, who had argued that commonwealths "by acquisition" were no less legitimate than commonwealths "by institution," as both result from agreements made out of fear.[13] Locke, by contrast, denies that promises extorted by force constitute genuine consent, and hence he concludes that conquest conveys "no lawful title" to rule.[14] Even after generations of foreign domination, a conquered people still retains the right to resist its rulers and seek its freedom. But a people's right to resistance is not limited to situations of rule by foreigners. Here is what Locke says immediately after raising the case of the Grecian Christians:

> For no government can have a right to obedience from a people who have not freely consented to it; which they can never be supposed to do, till either they are put in a full state of liberty to chuse their government and governors, or at least till they have such standing laws, to which they have by themselves or their representatives given their free consent, and also till they are allowed their due property, which is so to be proprietors of what they have, that no body can take away any part of it without their own consent, without which, men under any government are not in the state of freemen, but are direct slaves under the force of war.[15]

As a careful reading of this passage makes clear, its logic applies no less fully to people who are governed by rulers of their own nationality or religion than to those who are ruled by others. Thus it is not surprising that, in the concluding chapter of the *Second Treatise* ("Of the Dissolution of Government"), Locke formulates in a more general fashion his support for a right of resistance to arbitrary government—the "doctrine of a power in the people of providing for their safety a-new, by a new legislative, when their legislators have acted contrary to their trust, by invading their property." He even states explicitly that whether the rulers are foreigners or fellow nationals is irrelevant in this regard: "The peoples right is equally invaded, and their liberty lost, whether they are made slaves to any of their own, or a foreign nation; and in this lies the injury, and against this only have they the right of defence."[16] In upholding the people's right to revolt against a government that has betrayed (or never earned) its trust, Locke again decisively breaks with Hobbes, who held that "there can happen no breach of Covenant on the part of the Soveraigne; and consequently none of his Subjects, by any pretence of forfeiture, can be freed from his Subjection."[17]

But by what right can a particular group of human beings, in the first place, unite themselves in a community that separates them from their fellow human beings? Locke's answer is that this is something that "any number of men may do, because it injures not the freedom of the rest; they are left as they were in the liberty of the state of nature." The "bonds of civil society" are not natural but are put on voluntarily; precisely for that reason, those who mutually agree to live with these bonds have the right to do so. What they cannot justly do is to compel those who do not wish to be part of their community to become members. Locke insists that every human being enjoys the freedom and equality of the state of nature until he expressly agrees to join a commonwealth. "Nor is it now any more hindrance to the freedom of mankind, that they are born under constituted and ancient polities, that have established laws, and set forms of government, than if they were born in the woods, amongst the unconfined inhabitants, that run loose in them." Thus every human being who reaches adulthood has the choice of whether to remain a member of the commonwealth to which his parents belong or to seek his fortune elsewhere. For Locke, the right of emigration, understood in this way, is a fundamental human right. At the same time, however, other commonwealths have no obligation to admit such emigrants—or any other persons—to membership.[18]

RELATIONS AMONG STATES

What, then, is the relationship among the various particular commonwealths that men voluntarily agree to create? Locke (again following Hobbes) asserts that they are in the state of nature vis-à-vis one another. In fact, it is their condition that Locke adduces as the clearest answer to those who question whether the state of nature really exists: "since all princes and rulers of independent governments all through the world, are in a state of nature, it is plain the world never was, nor ever will be, without numbers of men in that state." It is true that "the leagues that have been made between several states and kingdoms, either expresly or tacitly disowning all claim and right to the land in the others possession, have, by common consent, given up their pretences to their natural common right, which originally they had to those countries, and so have, by positive agreement, settled a property amongst themselves, in distinct parts and parcels of the earth." Yet even those communities that are thus "in league with others" remain in the state of nature with respect to one another: "For it is not every compact that puts an end to the state of nature between men, but only this one of agreeing together mutually to enter into one community, and make one body politic."[19]

Locke never seems to entertain the possibility that these separate communities, even if they are linked within a league, will ever take the further step of voluntarily agreeing to become part of a single body politic. Much less does he consider the possibility of restoring through a world government the global human community that prevails in the state of nature. While the inconveniences of the state of nature drive individual human beings into society, they do not drive separate commonwealths into uniting to form a common body politic. This seems to be because the inconveniences of lacking a common authority and a common judge are not so great in the case of commonwealths. As Hobbes had put it, though rulers of particular commonwealths are in a state of nature vis-à-vis one another, "because they uphold thereby, the Industry of their Subjects; there does not follow from it, that misery, which accompanies the Liberty of particular men."[20]

At the very outset of the *Second Treatise*, Locke defines political power as "a right of making laws with penalties of death, and consequently all less penalties, for the regulating and preserving of property, and of employing the force of the community, in the execution of such laws and in the defence of the common-wealth from foreign injury; and all this only for the public good."[21] Such power is legitimate—and hence truly "political," as opposed to "despotical"—only where it rests on the consent of the people and aims at preserving their property and pursuing the public good. But such legitimate power can accomplish its ends only if it has behind it the united force of the community. Locke stresses the right of the commonwealth to impose the death penalty and to compel its citizens to risk death to defend it in war—and he does not, as Hobbes had done in the *Leviathan*, offer excuses for those who resist arrest or make allowances for those who refuse to fight because of "naturall timorousnesse."[22] For Locke, legitimate political power is much more restricted than for Hobbes in terms of its ends—it must respect the property of the people and pursue the public good—but so long as it sticks to the pursuit of those ends, it has more unlimited authority over its subjects. While force without right is illegitimate, right without force is ineffectual. It is only a properly constructed commonwealth that can combine force with right and thus save men from the defects of the state of nature.

This means, however, that in relations among separate commonwealths there is no way that force can reliably be aligned with right. Even if they reach agreements mutually recognizing one another's claims to their respective territories, particular commonwealths remain in the state of nature with respect to one another. Only an agreement to form a single community, and to obey a single, visible common power, can put an end to the state of nature. Thus for Locke international relations remain a realm where force will sometimes be wielded without right, and "in all states and conditions," he affirms, "the true remedy of force without authority, is to oppose force to it."[23]

This is not to say, however, that force alone should rule the relations among independent states. The doctrine that conquest gives no right to rule clearly poses an obstacle to aggressive territorial expansion of the part of states. This is further reinforced by Locke's argument that the rights of the victor, even in a just war, over the families and property of the vanquished are severely limited. More generally, Locke's frequent condemnation of taking property by force, as opposed to earning it through labor and industry, points in the direction of an international realm characterized more by commercial than by military interactions. Finally, as we have seen, Locke has no objection to independent states entering into agreements that help to regulate their mutual relations.

VARIETIES OF MULTILATERALISM

The American perspective on international politics, I would argue, remains fundamentally Lockean. According to what we may dub the Lockean/American view, all human beings are endowed with universal human rights, but these can be effectively guaranteed only within particular commonwealths. At least for those who belong to states governed on the basis of popular consent and respect for individual rights, the highest obligation of citizens is to the constitution and the laws of their country. While a state may enter into agreements with other states, this cannot detract from its prior obligation to its own fundamental laws and its own citizens.

Yet by recognizing the essential role of particular commonwealths in the protection of universal human rights, the Lockean view implicitly endorses the existence of a multiplicity of independent states. More than that, it recognizes the legitimacy of other states—*provided that they too are based on consent and respect the rights of their citizens*. Even with states whose governments are not based on the consent of the governed, it is possible and often even necessary to reach and to honor various kinds of agreements for practical ends. At the same time, however, it is very difficult to endorse the legitimacy of such governments when they oppress their own people.

On the Lockean/American view, the moral authority of multilateralism inevitably appears compromised if the decisions of a multilateral body are shaped by states that do not respect the rights of their own citizens. Thus when the government of a country like Sudan is reelected to the Human Rights Commission while it is apparently encouraging horrific abuses against its own citizens in Darfur, some Europeans may shrug it off as an inevitable outcome of UN regional politicking, but for many Americans it severely undermines whatever moral credibility such a body may possess. This is one reason why there has been growing support in the United States for the concept of a Community of Democracies—that is, a global multilateral body whose membership is restricted to democratic states.

This underlines a more general transatlantic difference in perceptions. Many Europeans identify multilateralism as such with democracy. They sometimes ask how the United States can claim to be a champion of democracy when it refuses to go along with the decisions of multilateral bodies. But from the Lockean/American perspective, there is no contradiction here. Decision making in most existing multilateral institutions is not based on democratic principles of representation, and many member states are not themselves internally democratic. Such institutions can and sometimes do arrive at decisions that are hostile to democracy (witness the UN Human Rights Commission), and most Americans regard democracy as a greater good than multilateralism.

This is not to suggest that Lockeans/Americans do not care what the rest of the world thinks of them. They are especially uneasy about being at odds with their democratic allies. But they are not particularly troubled by being isolated within multilateral institutions like the UN when they feel that their country is in the right.

From a Lockean/American perspective, the goal of a foreign policy aimed at promoting democracy and human rights is the coming to power of liberal democratic governments in as many nations as possible. I would say that this also tends to be the predominant outlook among democratic movements around the world, as can readily be observed when they meet together on occasions such as the biennial assembly of the World Movement for Democracy. These prodemocracy groups almost always have a strong belief that human rights and democratic government are universal goods that should be available to all, and they show a high degree of solidarity and support for one another's struggles. Yet they invariably view their own goal as the achievement of democracy in their own country, and the goal of their assistance and solidarity with others as the attainment of democracy in those other countries. Despite the universalism of its principles, the global democratic movement is emphatically national in its focus and in its structure.

It must be acknowledged that this is less true of the global human rights movement—or at least of some of its leaders in the advanced democracies. The latter typically put greater stress on achieving international agreements and standards than on achieving political change within countries. Human rights form the universalist side of liberal democracy, and thus it is not surprising that those who view themselves primarily as advocates of human rights are inclined to a more exclusively universalist outlook than those who view themselves primarily as advocates of democracy. In principle, one may say, as Locke's *Second Treatise* suggests, that all human beings should enjoy these rights as members of the human community. In practice, however, as the teaching of the *Second Treatise* also suggests, these rights are likely to be respected only in particular states that are accountable to their citizens. International standards are of limited help where they cannot be enforced. Today the most serious human rights abuses—including genocide—are invariably carried out by, or with the complicity of, a non-democratic government.

In many cases, the only way to stop such abuses is through the use of force. But where will that force come from? Only from the militaries of other states. Ultimately, it is national armies that must vindicate the cause of human rights. National armies certainly have shown that they can work in coalition, often under the aegis of multilateral organizations, but they too remain resolutely national in their structure and focus, precisely for the Lockean reasons we have discussed. Whatever other virtues multilateral organizations may possess, they do not appear able to attract soldiers to fight and die on their behalf.

GLOBALISM VERSUS INTERNATIONALISM

Let me conclude by returning to the distinction between the new globalism and the old liberal internationalism. The globalists are right about the fact that we are facing problems whose solutions often must transcend international boundaries. In an increasingly interconnected world, the need for international cooperation is greater than it ever has been. I think most Americans recognize this, and they are not reluctant about such international engagement—indeed, they often take the lead in it. Americans are no longer isolationist. But because of their commitment to Lockean principles, they will embrace international engagement only within certain limits. While Lockeans/Americans may accept the description of the globalists, they will not accept their prescription for mechanisms of global governance that bypass or minimize the role of national political orders.

This has something to do, of course, with the strength of Americans' devotion to their country. Yet American patriotism is focused not on blood and soil but on the Declaration of Independence and on the Constitution. It is adherence to these documents that has given Americans a government that protects their rights and reflects their wishes. They can be persuaded of the need for greater degrees of international cooperation in many areas, but not for approaches to global governance that evade or attempt to supersede their Constitutional order. Lockeans/Americans are not averse to multilateralism; in fact, I would say that they are naturally inclined to internationalism, but they are hostile to globalism. So to the extent that liberal internationalism really is giving way to globalism in today's multilateral institutions, the prospects are high that the United States will continue to find itself being accused of unilateralism.

IV

CONCLUSION

10

The Democratic Moment Revisited

The dramatic ending of the Cold War and the demise of the Soviet Union constituted a critical turning point in world history. That is what people sensed at the time, and subsequent developments have only confirmed it. In the second chapter of this volume, an essay originally written just after the failed coup of August 1991 had sealed the doom of the USSR, I reflected on the new world that the expiration of the Cold War had brought into being—"a world with one dominant principle of political legitimacy, democracy, and only one superpower, the United States." The central question posed in that essay was "how long can this, the democratic moment, last?" and I predicted that it would "endure at least for the remainder of the [twentieth] century." In 2007, it would be fair to say that the democratic moment still endures—yet there is a widespread feeling that its survival is more threatened today than ever before.

It is not that the overall numbers of democratically elected governments or of Free countries (as measured by Freedom House) have declined. In fact, Freedom House's survey of the state of democracy in 2006 shows that the number of Free countries in the world actually increased by one to a new high of 90, while the number of electoral democracies held firm at its peak of 123. Yet the accompanying analysis offered by Arch Puddington of Freedom House speaks darkly of a "stagnation" of freedom and emphasizes the predominantly negative trends visible below the surface measured by countries' freedom scores.[1] This analysis confirms what most people engaged in the work of promoting democracy intuitively sense—that their struggle is becoming more difficult and that their opponents are more energized and more brazen than at any point in recent decades. Supporters of democracy increasingly feel that they are being put on the defensive.

To repeat, then, there has not been anything like a "reverse wave" of democratization, with large numbers of countries reverting to unvarnished authoritarianism. What has been and is happening is much more complex. Numerous countries where dictatorships were ousted have moved only hesitantly and partially toward democracy. And some of these countries—variously labeled by political scientists as "semidemocracies" or "hybrid regimes" or "pseudodemocracies" or even "competitive authoritarian" regimes—now seem no longer to be making even slow progress toward democracy, but rather to be backsliding toward greater authoritarianism. The most notorious example of this latter category is Russia.

Another significant set of countries, while still under dictatorial rule, had seemed to be ripe for democratic gains, but such hopes have largely been disappointed. In the Middle East, despite lavish diplomatic attention and the rise to prominence of a new democratic discourse, significant progress on the ground is hard to find. China, while opening up its economy and offering its citizens much greater freedom in their personal lives, so far has largely avoided any meaningful political reform. Elsewhere, dictatorial regimes that have resisted any moves toward liberalization, ranging from Burma to Cuba to Turkmenistan to North Korea, have shown much greater staying power than many had expected back in the 1990s.

The current picture cannot be fully understood, however, without considering the shift in worldwide perceptions of the United States and the dramatic rise of anti-Americanism. In terms of military strength and global influence, there is no question that the United States remains the world's only superpower. And despite the numerous inconsistencies in its foreign policy, it continues to be—and even to be viewed as—the leading champion of democracy.[2] Yet there is little doubt that hostility to America has increased sharply over the past decade. Although the global rise in anti-Americanism began before the invasion of Iraq, the war and the bloody and trouble-filled occupation have seriously compounded the problem and also created new doubts about the effort to spread democracy.

The administration of George W. Bush has made the advance of democracy an unprecedentedly central focus of U.S. foreign policy. In his second inaugural address in January 2005, President Bush stated: "[I]t is the policy of the United States to seek and support the growth of democratic movements and institutions in every nation and culture, with the ultimate goal of ending tyranny in our world."[3] This sentence is repeated almost word for word at the very beginning of *The National Security Strategy of the United States*, in a paragraph that concludes by stating, "This is the best way to provide enduring security for the American people."[4]

President Bush's words in his second inaugural surely stirred the hearts of democrats around the world. Moreover, most Americans probably would agree that the advance of democracy will improve the security of the United

States and that it should remain a long-term goal of the country's foreign policy. Yet the idea of making democracy the highest priority of American foreign policy in the here and now proved exceedingly difficult to implement. Initial efforts to apply this policy yielded some promising results in 2005, especially in the Middle East, but by 2007 these gains had mostly faded or been undone, and the Bush administration was generally perceived, both at home and abroad, to be in retreat from its democracy-promotion agenda, especially in its dealings with such key countries as Egypt, Pakistan, and Russia.

The enormous difficulty the United States encountered in its efforts to help build democracy in Iraq also gave rise to second thoughts in some quarters about the benefits of democracy promotion. For one thing, it reinforced the tendency on the part of some observers to believe that the cultures of non-Western peoples, especially Arabs, were ill-suited to democracy. Also reinforced was the view that the "premature" introduction of elections in societies that lack strong institutions and the rule of law would be counterproductive. Finally, the fact that the attempt to foster democracy in Iraq was connected with the military mission that overthrew Saddam Hussein led many to conflate democracy promotion with "regime change" imposed by external force of arms. All these reactions encouraged skepticism with regard to an active policy of seeking to advance democracy.

DEMOCRATIC LEGITIMACY AND THE RISE OF ANTI-AMERICANISM

Yet despite all these setbacks and complications, democracy seemed to maintain its unrivaled global legitimacy as the only form of government befitting an advanced and successful nation. The prestige of the United States may have taken a nosedive, but the prestige of democracy continued to soar. Perhaps the clearest evidence of this is the endorsement and growing support of democracy by the world's leading regional and international organizations. The European Union has made democracy a condition of membership. The Organization for Security and Cooperation in Europe (OSCE) and the Council of Europe also are explicit in their attachment to the goal of democracy. The Organization of American States (OAS) has affirmed its commitment to democracy and put in place a mechanism for taking action when the constitutional order is interrupted in one of its member states. The Commonwealth has suspended members whose governments have violated democratic norms. Even the African Union (the successor to the Organization of African Unity or OAU) and the Association of Southeast Asian Nations (ASEAN), regional organizations that include nondemocratic member states and had traditionally been leery of any intervention in one another's domestic politics, have increasingly taken measures to support democracy.

The global organizations of the UN family also have embraced democracy, not just by endorsing it in principle, but by providing concrete assistance. The UN secretariat now includes an Electoral Assistance Division charged with helping member states to carry out free and fair elections. A new United Nations Democracy Fund has been established to provide grants to nongovernmental organizations working to promote democracy. The United Nations Development Programme lists "democratic governance" as the first of its five major areas of work in achieving the Millennial Development Goals adopted by 189 nations at the UN Millennium Summit in 2000. The World Bank, despite its primarily economic focus, has made "good governance" a central part of its work and has defined this in a way intended to strengthen democratic institutions and processes. Today there can be no doubt that democracy enjoys an official international seal of approval.[5]

Moreover, if one were to look for a competitor to democracy as a globally legitimate form of government, it is hard to know what that might be. The only explicit critiques of democracy that one can find today tend to come from spokesmen for the most extreme Islamist forces—al-Qaeda or the Taliban or the Islamic Republic of Iran—as even so-called moderate Islamists have increasingly adopted a more democratic discourse. (I will return shortly to a fuller discussion of the challenge posed by Islamism.) Unlike in the days of the Cold War, when there was significant political and intellectual sympathy in the West for communism, today there is negligible Western support for explicitly antidemocratic ideologies. Nor are there nondemocratic regimes that find enthusiastic ideological backers in democratic countries, as once did Stalin's Russia, or Mao's China, or Castro's Cuba, or the Sandinistas' Nicaragua.

This is not to suggest the absence of opposition to—and even more widespread dissatisfaction with—liberal democracy. In my 1991 essay on "The Democratic Moment," I affirmed Ken Jowitt's argument that "liberalism will always leave many human beings unsatisfied and hence will generate powerful antiliberal movements. The real question," I continued, "is whether any such movement can succeed in attaining the economic success and broad appeal necessary to compete successfully with liberalism." A decade and a half later, I would say that no *positive* movement of this kind has yet arisen. What we have seen instead is the rise of a *negative* movement: anti-Americanism.

The resurgence of anti-Americanism has been brilliantly analyzed by Ivan Krastev, who sees it as a manifestation of a period "when no universal alternative to democracy and the market is in play, but disappointment with democracy and the market is growing."[6] Anti-Americanism offers a vehicle through which various kinds of political forces, including some in Western

Europe and other democratic countries, can find a "respectable" way of expressing hostility to liberal democracy. Thus it can take very different forms in different countries. Indeed, Krastev suggests that it is more appropriate to speak of *anti-Americanisms* in the plural. For a number of regimes, opposition to American hegemony/imperialism is a key element of their popular support and claim to legitimacy.

This is perhaps clearest in the case of Hugo Chavez's Venezuela, a regime that is often described as "populist." This designation is also ascribed to a variety of other governments and political forces both in Latin America and in other regions of the world, especially Central Europe and Southeast Asia. Although scholars argue about the precise meaning and proper application of the term, populism is generally agreed to possess certain common features: an aggrandizement of executive power at the expense of the legislature and the judiciary; an attempt to weaken or co-opt independent forces in civil society and in the private sector; and a tendency to use the state to deliver immediate material benefits to voters, often at the cost of undermining longer-run economic prosperity. Populists also often display (along with anti-Americanism) an intense nationalism and a hostility to religious or ethnic minorities.

While I would not dispute that populism poses a real challenge to liberal democracy in many countries, I view it not as an ideological alternative but rather as a recurring malady of democracy. In order to ward off this disease, liberal democratic regimes will have to do a better job of fighting poverty and unemployment and of helping to generate broad-based economic growth. In many cases, these goals will be hard to achieve, so it will not be surprising if more new democracies succumb to the populist temptation, and if some even wind up slipping all the way back to authoritarianism. Yet while populism may indeed undermine individual liberal democracies, it is hard to imagine its triumph on a global scale. For where it does come to power for any considerable length of time, it is most unlikely to produce enduring prosperity and stability.

THE ISLAMIST THREAT

Although anti-Americanism is a key factor in the Middle East as well, the situation there is quite different due to the attraction of Islamist doctrines. In my 1991 essay I had identified "radical or fundamentalist Islam" as "probably the most vital alternative to democracy to be found anywhere today," noting that in many Muslim countries free elections might bring to power Islamists rather than democrats. At the same time, I doubted the possibility that fundamentalist Islam would present a serious *global* challenge to democracy, pointing in part to the Islamic Republic of Iran's political and economic failures and its apparent loss of revolutionary élan. Today, in the light of 9/11, the persisting damage being wrought by al-Qaeda and other Islamist terrorist groups, and the new assertiveness of Iran, this subject demands a fresh look.

The key proposition I advanced in "The Democratic Moment" was the following: "Democracy's preeminence can be seriously challenged only by an ideology with universalist aspirations that proves capable of coming to power in an economically advanced or militarily powerful nation." As regards Islamism, there can be no doubt that it has universalist aspirations. The question was whether it could come to power in an advanced nation (or propel a less developed country to that status) and serve as a model that other countries would wish to follow. So far, the nations where radical Islam has come to power, Iran, Afghanistan, and Sudan, have not become objects of emulation, even within the Muslim world. The Taliban was driven from power with the support of external forces, but its ouster was greeted with joy by most Afghans. Sudan has proven incapable of imposing its Islamist policies on the rebellious southern half of the country, and its government is not taken as a model by anyone.

Iran is a much more important country and a much more complicated story. In the early 1990s it was nursing its wounds from the Iran-Iraq War and seemed to be moving toward more moderate and inward-looking policies. Then, the election of Mohammad Khatami to the presidency in 1997 brought in its train an efflorescence of reformist forces. Suddenly the Iranian scene was filled with discourse about civil society and the rule of law, popular sentiment seemed to have turned against the Islamic regime, and it appeared the country might be a not implausible candidate for a democratic transition. But Islamist forces proved resilient, and the subsequent election of Mahmoud Ahmadinejad to the presidency in 2005 signaled a return to the hard-line revolutionary spirit that had initially animated the regime.

Iran is a fascinating case, and its evolution in the years ahead will matter not just for the future of democracy but for the shape of international politics more generally. It is a significant regional power blessed with substantial oil wealth, and its boldness and ideological fervor have made it a force to be reckoned with. Still, by world standards it does not count as an "economically advanced or militarily powerful nation," and it has few friends or imitators, even within its own region, and uncertain backing among its own people. A key question today, of course, is whether the acquisition of nuclear weapons would enable it to vault into the ranks of global powers. Or put differently, would a nuclear-armed Iran, despite its other weaknesses, count as a "militarily powerful nation"?

This raises a larger question about technology and military power that is also relevant in considering the impact of non-state actors such as al-Qaeda.

In "The Democratic Moment," reflecting upon the apparent judgment of Soviet leaders that their system could no longer compete in an arms race with the West, I had noted the seeming military advantage enjoyed by democracies due to their economic and technological superiority. In this connection, I had cited the observation of Adam Smith: "In modern war the great expense of firearms gives an evident advantage to the nation which can best afford that expense." But what if the very advance of technology were to alter this relationship by making the acquisition of tremendous destructive power relatively cheap and thus available to less wealthy countries? That in effect is what nuclear proliferation represents. And while a nuclear-armed Iran (or North Korea) would not be in a position to wage a successful war against major world powers, it might be able to exert disproportionate influence on the international scene.

Thinking about the potential threat from al-Qaeda or other non-state actors raises the issue of technology in an even more acute form. The 9/11 attacks, of course, did enormous damage, and terrorism poses serious dangers in many parts of the world. Yet so long as terrorists are restricted to the use of conventional weapons, they do not pose a fundamental threat to the primacy of democracy. If they should be able, however, to obtain and successfully deliver weapons of mass destruction, the nature of the problem would be dramatically transformed, with potentially profound effects on national and international politics and on the course of world history.

Francis Fukuyama, in a passage from his famous article "The End of History?" that I quoted in 1991, asserted, "Our task is not to answer exhaustively the challenges to liberalism promoted by every crackpot messiah around the world, but only those that are embedded in important social or political forces and movements, and which are therefore part of world history." Yet a "crackpot messiah" who can acquire sufficiently potent weapons may well be able to force himself onto the stage of world history, even if he has only a small following. The way in which further technological advance could alter the equation can be illustrated by a thought experiment: Let us imagine the invention of a tiny device, capable of being easily concealed in one's pocket, that could destroy vast populations. Whoever possessed and was willing to use such a device would have enormous political power, if only for destructive purposes. In such a case, it would hardly matter what the "ideology" behind this "movement" was, or whether it was capable of embedding itself in wider social or political forces or staking a plausible claim to legitimacy. In effect, the situation would resemble the "mad scientist" scenario familiar to us from bad science fiction movies—one that democracies are particularly ill-suited to dealing with (at least in the absence of superheroes).

Thankfully, we have not arrived at this point yet, and the future of technology, which can bring advances that benefit the "defense" as well as the "offense," is notoriously hard to predict. When George Orwell wrote *1984*, it was widely feared that advances in communications technology would strengthen dictatorship and make the truth impossible to discern. A half-century later, the Internet and the cell phone were being celebrated as instruments of freedom that would help oppressed populations to gain access to the truth and to organize their liberation. Still, there does seem to be a strong prospect that technological advance will give influence to ideologies, groups, and individuals that would not otherwise be capable of commanding the adherence of large numbers of followers and of governing successfully—the traditional prerequisites for making a mark on world history. This is why Islamic fundamentalism may yet pose a much greater threat to the global hegemony of democracy than I had initially believed.

SOURCES OF COMPETITION

If Iran and Islamist terrorism pose the gravest unconventional threats to democratic societies, based on the combination of ideological fervor and willingness to use any means of destroying the West, other competitors to democracy are also discernible. The most prominent of these are China and Russia, the two most powerful nondemocratic countries in the world today. In my 1991 essay, I had emphasized their "decisive importance for the future of democracy," arguing that a "reinvigorated communism" was extremely unlikely, but that neoauthoritarianism was as likely an outcome in these two countries as stable democracy. China and Russia have followed very different trajectories over the intervening years, so let me discuss each in turn.

In the aftermath of the 1989 Tiananmen massacre, China has been remarkably successful in achieving impressively high economic growth, maintaining political stability, and reinserting itself into the global order. Given its huge population, if it continues to become richer at anything like its present pace, China will before long become an economic and military power of the first rank. The country's rapidly increasing prosperity is due in large measure to market-oriented policies and integration with the world economy. This approach has been accompanied by a dramatic increase in personal freedom for those who steer clear of politics (and certain kinds of religious activities). Yet it has remained a one-party dictatorship, with the ruling Chinese Communist Party (CCP) maintaining stringent constraints on political organization and expression.

The central question raised by China's progress, of course, is how long this combination of economic openness and political repression can continue to work: Is there some point at which the perpetuation of high levels of economic growth will become incompatible with existing political controls? After all, there are a number of examples of developing countries that have achieved extraordinary growth rates under authoritarian rule, but among advanced economies only tiny Singapore is not a democracy. Experience elsewhere suggests that, at some point, rising middle classes demand political as well as personal freedom. Moreover, the lack of democracy is inevitably accompanied by failings in transparency, accountability, and the rule of law that, as countries become more developed, threaten to cripple their economic performance. The question, however, is when (if at all) China will reach the point where these contradictions become acute enough to produce either economic distress or a political breakthrough. I believe that without democratic reform China's economic progress will eventually hit a wall—but I have been believing this for some time now, and it has not happened yet. So a key question for the future of democracy is whether China will be able to continue its economic rise without democratizing.

One reason that I believe China will face grave difficulties in the years ahead is the disjunction between its communist principle of legitimacy, which is used to justify CCP rule, and the real bases of its current "postcommunist" economic system. It is almost universally accepted that, while the CCP still rules in largely Leninist fashion, few of its rulers and even fewer of its subjects are seriously committed to Marxist doctrine, and that in practice the country has moved a long way toward capitalism. It is frequently argued that the rule of the CCP today is, instead, based on some combination of Chinese nationalism and the "performance legitimacy" that derives from its record of bringing growing prosperity to the country. Some analysts have contended that, with communism having been reduced to a negligible factor in the life and governance of the country, the CCP soon will simply change its name and officially adopt some kind of nationalist ideology. I have always been skeptical about the willingness or capacity of the CCP to take this step. It is quite rare and never easy for a regime to fundamentally alter the principles on which it bases its claim to legitimacy. Moreover, in an era where multipartism and elections remain the global norm, I do not see how, in the absence of communist doctrine, the CCP can plausibly justify rule by a single party that refuses to allow political competition.

China is exerting growing influence around the world, but its "footprint" is especially heavy in East and Southeast Asia, where both its actions and its example create significant obstacles to further democratization in the region. One also hears a great deal about the "Chinese model" these days in Africa, the Middle East, and Latin America, but there is very little real substance to this talk. Generally, the "Chinese model" is understood simply as market reform accompanied by undemocratic rule. No doubt many authoritarian regimes would like to make this combination work, but few are able to do so. And none of them appear to be rushing to adopt Chinese-style political institutions or to establish formal one-party rule.

Nonetheless, if China is able to continue its extraordinary economic growth without democratizing and becomes a second superpower, it obviously will pose a potential global danger to democracy. If one thinks in terms of the traditional great-power politics that have shaped the course of world politics in the past, China is clearly the leading threat to democracy's global hegemony.

As for Russia, it is now generally acknowledged that it is not—or no longer is—a democracy. (Freedom House demoted it to the ranks of Not Free states in 2004.) There remains a lively debate about whether it had in fact been a democracy under the presidency of Boris Yeltsin (1992–1999). For those who argue that the Yeltsin years were essentially authoritarian, it is easier to contend that the Putin years represent progress on a slow and winding road toward democracy. In my own view, however, Putin's rule has witnessed the amassing of more and more power in the hands of the executive and the emasculation of whatever independent forces remained—all of which adds up to unmistakable backsliding with regard to democracy. The failure to bring Russia into the democratic fold has been the gravest setback for democracy of the post–Cold War era.

It is very hard to characterize the precise nature of the current Russian regime. Despite the ever-growing centralization of power in a "superpresidency," the regime retains at least some of the trappings of democracy, and the gaining of office through elections (however unfair and manipulated these may be) still seems to be an essential pillar of its legitimacy. For this reason, the problem of succession promises to be the Achilles heel of the new Russian system. There are few cases of authoritarian regimes that have succeeded in imposing strict term limits for their highest office—Mexico under the PRI is a striking example, but it featured a deeply institutionalized ruling party of the kind that the Russian regime does not appear to be interested in creating. The coming year will reveal whether Putin can avoid the temptation (and the pleadings of many of his associates) to run for a currently unconstitutional third term. If he chooses not to run, the system will be sorely tested by the change at the top, with consequences that are exceedingly difficult to predict.

Putin and some of his advisors have labeled the system they have created "managed democracy" or (more recently) "sovereign democracy." The latter term seems to underline a firm resistance to having other countries tell Russia how it should govern itself or what standards it should adhere to, and this stance obviously is in accord with the nationalist, xenophobic, and anti-Western attitudes that the regime has fostered. At the same time, Putin has not appealed to "Russian exceptionalism" or some kind of ideology based on Russia's unique religious and historical roots. Although some analysts see "managed democracy" as a serious attempt at developing a model that combines elite management with popular backing, I remain unconvinced that there is a coherent ideology at work here, as opposed to a superficial rationalization of the amassing of power and wealth by Putin and his cronies.

Moreover, the growing prosperity that has helped keep Putin popular with the Russian people has been tied in large part to high oil prices. If oil prices decline or even just fail to continue rising, there is likely to be a sharp falling off in support for the regime. If this should happen when an untried successor to Putin has taken office, the prospect of political instability will be especially high. The underlying demographic and economic trends in Russia are far from favorable. The country's population is declining due to low birth rates, poor health care, and appalling mortality rates. And in tying its economic future so tightly to oil and gas revenues, it has failed to develop its capabilities in other areas. In sum, the dangers to democracy posed by Russia are more likely to flow from the country's weakness than from the success of its model.

In my essay on "The Democratic Moment," I had cited Japan as a third "country to watch," on the grounds that it (along with the other rapidly developing noncommunist countries of East Asia) might become the source of a kind of "neo-Confucian" ideology hostile to liberal democracy. This worry, at least so far, has not been realized. Despite an extended period of economic stagnation, Japan has remained firmly in the democratic camp. Moreover, both Korea and Taiwan not only completed successful transitions to democracy but moved away from the "dominant-party" democracy long characteristic of Japan, as each experienced closely fought party competition and alternation of power. The balance in Asia also has been shifted by the democratic transition in Indonesia, the most populous country in Southeast Asia and formerly a strong advocate of distinctively "Asian values." More generally, the 1998 Asian financial crisis undermined the notion that Asia was developing an economic and political model superior to that of Western democracy. There are still reasons for concern about how deeply democracy has taken root in the region, ranging from the 2006 coup in Thailand to the persistence of "authoritarian nostalgia" in Korea and Taiwan, but it no longer seems plausible to expect that the region's noncommunist states will develop a distinctive ideological model of their own.

Finally, note must be taken of a country that went unmentioned in "The Democratic Moment," but today looms much larger on the world scene—namely, India. Projected to overtake China as the world's most populous country sometime in the next half-century, India has long stood out as an exception to the view that stable and enduring democracy could not take hold in poor countries. What is new is that, since it began adopting more open and market-friendly economic policies in the early 1990s, it has begun to grow at a much more rapid pace and has become a significant player in the world economy. If India is able to maintain its new economic dynamism, it could be a critically important factor strengthening the democratic cause, especially as a counterweight and counterexample to a growing but still undemocratic China.

THE STATE OF THE WEST

Having now examined "the rest," it is time to look at the state of the West, and in particular at the two long-standing bastions of liberal democracy in the world—Europe and the United States. Europe was seemingly the great beneficiary of the end of the Cold War. Divided for more than four decades by the "Iron Curtain," the continent today is indeed "whole and free" (at least up to the western borders of the former Soviet Union). All the former Warsaw Pact countries have now been successfully incorporated into the European Union. Yet despite these remarkable gains, a dark cloud seems to hang over Europe. The defeat of the new EU Constitution in referenda in both France and the Netherlands in 2005 brought to a sudden halt the sense of European momentum toward "ever greater union." The real significance of the Constitutional setback was not that truly far-reaching changes were stymied (in fact, the proposed changes were modest and incremental), but that European citizens in the core countries of the EU indicated their unhappiness with the political structure being built in their name.

While Europeans are dissatisfied with the European Union's "democratic deficit," they also seem increasingly doubtful about the effectiveness of their national governments—in part because a good deal of the authority and capacity of the latter has been drifting toward Brussels. Moreover, after the impressive exertions involved in bringing in twelve new member states between 2004 and 2007, the EU is experiencing a sense of "enlargement fatigue," and its expansionist dynamism is clearly waning. Europe's overall economic performance has fallen short of that of many other parts of the world. Its impending demographic decline not only imperils its generous welfare states, but threatens to diminish its overall global importance. Its below-replacement-level fertility rates mean that it is likely to continue attracting large-scale immigration, much of it from its Muslim neighbors. The riots and bombings of recent years indicate that it will face serious and growing problems in integrating its Muslim populations. And the EU seems no closer than before to being able to forge a common foreign policy.

In "The Democratic Moment," I did not directly focus on Europe; if I had, I doubt if I would have raised any concerns about the stability of democracy in Western Europe. Today, however, I am not so sure that the future of democracy in Europe is secure. If democracy were to unravel even in a single EU country, the psychological damage to the global democratic cause would be very serious indeed. Fortunately, the European Union (even if it may indirectly be weakening to some extent the national democracies of its member states) offers a strong bulwark for resisting such a development. Moreover, Europe's alliance with the United States also provides it with some cushion against democratic backsliding.

In 1991, I had concluded my essay on "The Democratic Moment" by expressing concern about the health of American democracy. In 2007, I am more optimistic in this regard. Certainly, the United States has experienced some difficult times since then, and today, in the midst of what increasingly appears to be an unsuccessful war in Iraq, American politics is extraordinarily polarized and bitter. Yet while Americans may be deeply divided, it is within a quite narrow political spectrum. There remains an unchallenged and unshakeable consensus in support of liberal democracy and a strong sense of national cohesion. On the whole, relations among different races and ethnic groups have been improving. The United States seems much better able than European nations to integrate minority groups. It has chalked up a successful record of economic growth and kept both unemployment and inflation quite low. And while the U.S. welfare state, like its European counterparts, will suffer the pressures created by an aging population, the United States does not face the prospect of an overall demographic decline.

A strong alliance between Europe and the United States is clearly vital to the global fortunes of democracy, but as the events of recent years have shown, this is not always easy to maintain. While the style and some of the specific policies of the Bush administration have exacerbated transatlantic frictions, I believe that the underlying causes of these tensions lie in political and cultural differences between the two sides that will not be resolved simply by a change at the helm in the United States. On the other hand, these differences are not all that deep, for at the most profound level Europeans and Americans share a common commitment to liberal democracy and the way of life it makes possible. (One sign of this is that European leaders, despite their hostility to the U.S. war in Iraq, have not turned against the idea of democracy promotion but have embraced it, highlighting the EU's own contributions and achievements in this area.[7]) Because of their common commitment to liberal democracy, Europeans and Americans share common interests. They will ultimately feel threatened by the same enemies, even if they may often disagree about the best methods for dealing with them. As long as liberal democracy continues to prevail within Europe, no unbridgeable rift is likely to develop between the two sides of the Atlantic.

The most significant divergences between the United States and Europe relate to their differing appraisals not of liberal democracy but of the nation-state. For many Europeans, the overriding lesson of the Second World War was the dangers of nationalism and the need to tame it. For Americans, by contrast, the chief lesson was the danger of allowing tyrannical power to grow unchecked. For both sides, the remedies for these dangers were seen to include heightened international cooperation as well as the strengthening and spread of liberal democracy, yet the European tendency has been to emphasize the first and the American to emphasize the second. The same divergence has been evident in their responses to the phenomenon of globalization.

As I have argued earlier in this volume, the implications of globalization have frequently been exaggerated or misread, particularly with respect to the future of the nation-state and of democracy. The notion of a borderless world remains a fantasy. If it were to become a reality, however, the consequences for democracy would be dire. Thus the goal of friends of liberal democracy should be not to supersede the nation-state but to make it more amenable to the requisite international cooperation. In my view, this cannot be accomplished by undercutting the nation-state. It requires the development of forms of multilateralism that make it possible for strong nation-states to work effectively together when common goals and problems demand it.

Although nation-states will always have conflicting interests, liberal democracies have proven themselves better able to live in peace with one another and to foster international cooperation than other kinds of regimes. This is one more reason why the spread of liberal democracy is to be desired. It is nondemocratic regimes that pose the greatest dangers to international peace and cooperation.

In a mere two centuries liberal democracy has progressed from a new and rare form of government to the dominant type of regime in the world. One effect of the growing ideological hegemony of democracy has been gradually to weaken older principles of legitimacy that in the past provided the basis for relatively decent if imperfect regimes. Increasingly, the world is divided between liberal democracies (or regimes that are striving or pretending to be liberal democracies) and regimes that are tyrannical or are tending in that direction. This is a further reason why the global advance of democracy is a more compelling goal than ever before.

THE FUTURE OF DEMOCRACY PROMOTION

None of this means that democracy promotion is a "magic bullet" that can solve the problems of international relations. This is especially true because democracy promotion is so difficult an enterprise and so uncertain of success. The lessons of Afghanistan and Iraq only confirm what the postcolonial experience of the 1950s and 1960s should already have taught us. It is one thing to establish democratic institutions; it is something entirely different and infinitely harder to make them work. For most of human history popular self-government has been quite rare. Today it has spread much more widely than ever before, but that should not lead us to underestimate its difficulty. Moreover, there are severe limits on what outsiders can do to nurture liberal democracy in other lands. In any case, given the imperatives of national security and national interests, no state is in a position to make promoting democracy the most urgent item on its foreign policy agenda. In consequence, it is wise to be modest in our claims of what democracy promotion can achieve and of how unswervingly any nation can pursue it.

This is not to suggest that democracy promotion is a kind of fad, a peculiar artifact of the post–Cold War period destined soon to fade into oblivion. As a consequence of democracy's still unrivaled legitimacy, efforts to promote it are unlikely to recede any time soon. Consider the issue of "post-conflict" states. These may be the product of external invasion, as in the cases of Afghanistan and Iraq, but more often they have been the result of civil wars. Typically, the attempt to reconstruct them has been taken up by the international community under the aegis of the United Nations, as in the cases of Haiti, Mozambique, Cambodia, Bosnia, Sierra Leone, East Timor, Kosovo, and Liberia. In addition to having undergone the trauma of civil war, most of these countries are desperately poor or riven by ethnic conflict. None of them would be considered a very promising candidate for popular self-government. And yet democracy building has been an integral component of the international reconstruction effort in all these places. Why?

Part of the explanation is that elections can be a useful mechanism for resolving long-standing civil conflicts; exhausted combatants on both sides may be willing to trust their fate to a free and fair election, especially if there are some guarantees for the losers. But the more important factor lies in the legitimacy democracy enjoys in the international community. Both the international organizations and the great powers that have taken the lead in responding to postconflict situations would find it exceedingly awkward to evade their proclaimed commitment to democracy in a jurisdiction under their protection. These days one cannot imagine a U.S. president justifying—or U.S. public opinion accepting—a decision to hand over a territory under U.S. control to an unelected authoritarian leader. And although the UN readily accommodates authoritarian regimes among its member states, it too feels compelled to try to leave behind functioning democratic institutions in places where it takes responsibility for postconflict situations.

Building democratic institutions under such inhospitable conditions is a task fraught with complications. Restoring peace and security and rebuilding the state in postconflict situations demands a whole array of capabilities and resources that go far beyond the demands of democracy assistance in more settled conditions. Yet, especially because of the worldwide focus on Iraq and Afghanistan, public opinion increasingly tends to identify democracy promotion with these exceedingly hard cases. Given the disturbing state of affairs in Iraq and the emerging signs of regression in Afghanistan, the growing skepticism about democracy promotion in some quarters is not surprising. Yet the appeal and the advantages of democracy assistance in more ordinary situations (including its relatively low cost) are so compelling that it is not likely to be abandoned.

It is much easier today than it was in 1991 to spin out scenarios that would lead to a global retreat from democracy in the decades ahead. Such scenarios might feature a growth in the political influence and destructive power (via nuclear proliferation and terrorism) of radical Islam, the continuing rise of an authoritarian China, a backsliding from democracy in parts of Europe, or a turn toward isolationism in the United States following a failure in Iraq. It is also possible to imagine a further increase in anti-Americanism that undermines the global legitimacy of democracy. For there is something anomalous about the exalted prestige of democracy coexisting with the widespread denigration of the United States, and it is hard to see how this disjunction can long persist. Any or all of these unhappy scenarios are possible, yet liberal democracy has enormous assets on its side. Even apart from the powerful attractions of individual freedom and self-government, democracy is still the only type of regime that has proven itself capable of delivering to advanced societies high levels of prosperity and stable governance. So if I had to venture a judgment today about the likely state of the world in 2020, I would predict that the democratic moment that began in 1991 will still endure.

Notes

CHAPTER ONE

1. Amartya Sen, "Democracy as a Universal Value," *Journal of Democracy* 10 (July 1999): 3–17, 4.

2. Adrian Karatnycky, "A Century of Progress," *Journal of Democracy* 11 (January 2000): 187–200.

3. Sen, "Democracy as a Universal Value," 5.

4. Ronald Reagan, Address to the British Parliament, 8 June 1982, available at www.historyplace.com/speeches/reagan-parliament.htm.

5. Marc F. Plattner and Larry Diamond, "Why the 'Journal of Democracy,'" *Journal of Democracy* 1 (Winter 1990): 3–5.

6. Marc F. Plattner and Larry Diamond, "Democracy's Future," *Journal of Democracy* 6 (January 1995): 3–6, 4.

7. Plattner and Diamond, "Democracy's Future," 4.

8. Plattner and Diamond, "Democracy's Future," 4.

9. Plattner and Diamond, "Democracy's Future," 5.

10. Larry Diamond, "Is the Third Wave Over?" *Journal of Democracy* 7 (July 1996): 20–37.

11. Fareed Zakaria, "The Rise of Illiberal Democracy," *Foreign Affairs* 76 (November–December 1997): 22–43.

12. Zakaria, "The Rise of Illiberal Democracy," 23.

13. Benjamin Constant, "The Liberty of the Ancients Compared with That of the Moderns" in Benjamin Constant, *Political Writings*, ed. and translated by Biancamaria Fontana (Cambridge: Cambridge University Press, 1988), 308–29.

14. Constant, "The Liberty of the Ancients Compared with That of the Moderns," 311–12.

15. Constant, "The Liberty of the Ancients Compared with That of the Moderns," 312.

16. Edward D. Mansfield and Jack Snyder, "Democratization and the Danger of War," *International Security* 20 (Summer 1995): 5–38; Edward D. Mansfield and Jack Snyder, *Electing to Fight: Why Emerging Democracies Go to War* (Cambridge: MIT Press, 2005); Amy Chua, *World on Fire: How Exporting Free Market Democracy Breeds Ethnic Hatred and Global Instability* (New York: Doubleday, 2003).

17. Thomas Carothers, "How Democracies Emerge: The 'Sequencing' Fallacy," *Journal of Democracy* 18 (January 2007): 12–27.

18. John Ruggie, "Territoriality and Beyond: Problematizing Modernity in International Relations," *International Organization* 47 (Winter 1993): 139–74.

19. Juan J. Linz and Alfred Stepan, *Problems of Democratic Transition and Consolidation: Southern Europe, South America, and Post-Communist Europe* (Baltimore: Johns Hopkins University Press, 1996), 28.

20. Benjamin Barber, "2001 Introduction: Terrorism's Challenge to Democracy," *Jihad vs. McWorld: How Globalism and Tribalism Are Reshaping the World* (London: Corgi, 2003), xxiii.

21. Barber, *Jihad vs. McWorld*, xxiv.

22. Marc F. Plattner, "Building Democracy after Conflict: Introduction," *Journal of Democracy* 16 (January 2005): 5–8.

CHAPTER TWO

1. Daniel P. Moynihan, "The American Experiment," *The Public Interest* 41 (Fall 1975): 6–7.

2. Francis Fukuyama, "The End of History?" *The National Interest* 16 (Summer 1989): 3–18.

3. Miklós Haraszti, "A Choice Between Resolution and Emotion," *East European Reporter* (Spring–Summer 1990): 76.

4. See Seymour Martin Lipset, "The Death of the Third Way," *The National Interest* 20 (Summer 1990): 25–37.

5. Milan Šimečka, "The Restoration of Freedom," *Journal of Democracy* 1 (Summer 1990): 3–12.

6. *Washington Post*, 31 March 1991, A23.

7. Interview with Václav Klaus, *NFF Update* (Winter 1991): 2.

8. Adam Smith, *The Wealth of Nations*, 2 vols. (Chicago: University of Chicago Press, 1976), 2:230.

9. Ken Jowitt, "The New World Disorder," *Journal of Democracy* 2 (Winter 1991): 11–20.

10. Samuel P. Huntington, "Democracy's Third Wave," *Journal of Democracy* 2 (Spring 1991): 27.

CHAPTER THREE

1. Thomas Hobbes, *Leviathan*, ed. by C. B. Macpherson (London: Penguin Books, 1985).

2. Spinoza, Benedict de. "Theologico-Political Treatise," in *Works of Spinoza* vol. 1, trans. by R. H. M. Elwes (New York: Dover, 1951).

3. John Locke, *Second Treatise of Government*, ed. by C. B. Macpherson (Indianapolis: Hackett, 1980).

4. Alexander Hamilton, James Madison, and John Jay, *The Federalist Papers*, ed. by Clinton Rossiter (New York: New American Library, 1961).

5. Immanuel Kant, "Perpetual Peace," in *Kant on History*, ed. and trans. by Lewis White Beck (Indianapolis: Bobbs-Merrill, 1963).

6. Jean-Jacques Rousseau, *The Social Contract* (Baltimore: Penguin Books, 1968), bk. I, ch. 8, p. 65.

7. Immanuel Kant, *Foundations of the Metaphysics of Morals*, ed. and trans. Lewis White Beck (Indianapolis: Bobbs-Merrill, 1959).

8. Andrei Sakharov, *Trialogue* magazine, 1979, cited in *Journal of Democracy* 1 (Spring 1990): 38.

CHAPTER FOUR

1. Samuel P. Huntington, *The Third Wave: Democratization in the Late Twentieth Century* (Norman, OK: University of Oklahoma Press, 1991).

2. Larry Diamond, "Is the Third Wave Over?" *Journal of Democracy* 7 (July 1996): 20–37.

3. Samuel P. Huntington, "After Twenty Years: The Future of the Third Wave," *Journal of Democracy* 8 (October 1997): 3–12.

4. Fareed Zakaria, "The Rise of Illiberal Democracy," *Foreign Affairs* 76 (November–December 1997): 22–43.

5. John Locke, *Second Treatise of Government*, ed. by C. B. Macpherson (Indianapolis: Hackett, 1980), ch. 2, sec. 4, p. 8.

6. Alexander Hamilton, James Madison, and John Jay, *The Federalist Papers*, ed. by Clinton Rossiter (New York: New American Library, 1961), no. 10, pp. 77–84.

7. Hamilton, Madison, and Jay, *The Federalist Papers*, no. 63, p. 387.

8. Jean-Jacques Rousseau, *The Social Contract* (Baltimore: Penguin Books, 1968), bk. III, ch. 15, p. 143.

9. Hamilton, Madison, and Jay, *The Federalist Papers*, no. 10, p. 82.

10. Aristotle, *Politics*, trans. and with an intro. by Carnes Lord (Chicago: University of Chicago Press, 1985), p. 131 (1294b).

11. Montesquieu, *De l'esprit des lois*, bk. II, ch. 2, translation mine.

12. John Stuart Mill, *Considerations on Representative Government*, ed. and with intro. by Currin V. Shields (New York: Liberal Arts Press, 1958), 127–47.

13. Mill, *Considerations on Representative Government*, 56–67.

14. Rousseau, *The Social Contract*, bk. II, ch. 6, p. 82 and bk. III, ch. 8, p. 124.

15. Bilahari Kausikan, "Hong Kong, Singapore, and 'Asian Values': Governance that Works," *Journal of Democracy* 8 (April 1997): 24–34.

CHAPTER FIVE

1. Fareed Zakaria, "The Rise of Illiberal Democracy," *Foreign Affairs* 76 (November–December 1997): 22–43.

2. John Locke, *Second Treatise of Government*, ed. by C. B. Macpherson (Indianapolis: Hacket, 1980), ch. 2, sec. 4, p. 8.

3. John Locke, *First Treatise*, in Peter Laslett, ed., *Two Treatises of Government* (New York: New American Library, 1960), ch. 1, sec. 5, p. 178.

4. Locke, *Second Treatise*, ch. 8, sec. 95, p. 52.

5. Locke, *Second Treatise*, ch. 19, sec. 222, p. 111.

6. Locke, *Second Treatise*, ch. 10, sec. 132, p. 68.

7. Locke, *Second Treatise*, ch. 19, sec. 223, p. 113.

8. Locke, *Second Treatise*, ch. 19, sec. 223, pp. 112–13.

9. Alexander Hamilton, James Madison, and John Jay, *The Federalist Papers*, ed. by Clinton Rossiter (New York: New American Library, 1961), no. 39, p. 240.

10. S. MacCoby, ed., *The English Radical Tradition, 1763–1914* (London: Nicholas Kaye, 1952), 31–32, 36, 39–40.

11. Thomas Paine, *Dissertation on First Principles of Government*, in Nelson F. Adkins, ed., *Common Sense and Other Political Writings* (New York: Liberal Arts Press, 1953), 155–74. All quotes from Paine come from this work.

12. James Mill, *An Essay on Government* (Indianapolis: Bobbs-Merrill, 1955). All quotes come from ch. 8, pp. 72–82.

13. Thomas Babington Macaulay, "Mill on Government," in *The Works of Lord Macaulay* (New York: Hurd and Houghton, 1878), 2:5–51. All quotes from Macaulay are taken from this essay.

14. Alexis de Tocqueville, *Democracy in America*, ed. Phillips Bradley (New York: Vintage, 1960) 2:270.

15. Tocqueville, *Democracy in America*, 1:59.

16. Gertrude Himmelfarb, *Victorian Minds* (New York: Harper & Row, 1970), 348.

17. James Fitzjames Stephen, *Liberty, Equality, Fraternity* (Cambridge: Cambridge University Press, 1967), pp. 210–12. This and subsequent quotes from Stephen are drawn from ch. 5, pp. 179–229.

18. John Stuart Mill occupies a curious place in the evolution of thinking about extension of the suffrage. In his *Considerations on Representative Government* (1861), he argues that "it is a personal injustice to withhold from anyone, unless for the prevention of greater evils, the ordinary privilege of having his voice reckoned in the disposal of affairs in which he has the same interest as other people." He not only opposes property qualifications, but vehemently rejects his father James Mill's argument for denying the suffrage to women. Nonetheless, he defends denying the vote to illiterates, those who pay no taxes, and those on relief. Moreover, he not only accepts these exceptions in practice to universal suffrage, but explicitly rejects the very principle of *equal* suffrage. Today his argument in favor of awarding multiple votes to those possessing "individual mental superiority" (as indicated by their profession or educational attainments) seems even more archaic than arguments for restricting the suffrage. See John Stuart Mill, *Considerations on Representative Government* (New York: Liberal Arts Press, 1958), 127–47.

19. On the spread of judicial review, see Nathan Brown, "Judicial Review and the Arab World" and Herman Schwartz, "Eastern Europe's Constitutional Courts," *Journal of Democracy* 9 (October 1998): 85–114.

20. On the rise of these institutions, see Andreas Schedler, Larry Diamond, and Marc F. Plattner, eds., *The Self-Restraining State: Power and Accountability in New Democracies* (Boulder, CO.: Lynne Rienner, 1999).

CHAPTER SIX

1. Jean-Jacques Rousseau, *Emile*, trans., Allan Bloom (New York: Basic Books, 1979), 453.

2. Thomas L. Friedman, *The Lexus and the Olive Tree* (New York: Farrar, Straus, and Giroux, 1999), xiii–xiv.

3. Samuel P. Huntington, *The Third Wave: Democratization in the Late Twentieth Century* (Norman, OK: University of Oklahoma Press, 1991), 26.

4. Amartya Sen, "Democracy as a Universal Value," *Journal of Democracy* 10 (July 1999): 5.

5. The election to the presidency of hard-line conservative Mahmoud Ahmadinejad in 2005, three years after the initial publication of this essay, clearly marked a reversal of reformist and prodemocratic trends in Iran, though there is still reason to believe that significant unhappiness with the clerical regime persists among the Iranian people.

6. In 2006, four years after the initial publication of this essay, the Thai army carried out a coup against the government of Prime Minister Thaksin Shinawatra. Though many Thai democrats were alarmed at Thaksin's authoritarian tendencies, and some at least tacitly welcomed the coup, it must nonetheless be counted as a serious setback for democracy in Thailand.

7. For a general account of this development, see Roland Rich, "Bringing Democracy into International Law," *Journal of Democracy* 12 (July 2001): 20–23.

8. Larry Diamond, "Is the Third Wave Over?" *Journal of Democracy* 7 (July 1996): 20–37; Samuel P. Huntington, "After Twenty Years: The Future of the Third Wave," *Journal of Democracy* 8 (October 1997): 3–12; Fareed Zakaria, "The Rise of Illiberal Democracy," *Foreign Affairs* 76 (November–December 1997): 22–43.

9. John Locke, *Second Treatise of Government*, ed. C. B. Macpherson. (Indianapolis: Hackett, 1980), ch. 8, sec. 95, p. 52.

10. Locke, *Second Treatise,*, ch. 9, sec. 123–24, p. 66.

11. Montesquieu, *De l'esprit des lois*, bk. XX, ch. 7; book XXI, ch. 20 (translations mine).

12. Ralf Dahrendorf, "Can European Democracy Survive Globalization?" *The National Interest* (Fall 2001): 20.

13. This concern is echoed by Dahrendorf, who calls the EU's decision-making process "an insult to democracy." As he notes, "The Union has now laid down very serious tests of democratic virtue for so-called accession countries. If, however, it applied these tests to itself, the Union, the results would be dismal. It is not just a joke to say that if the EU itself applied for accession to the EU it could not be admitted because it is insufficiently democratic." Ralf Dahrendorf, "Can European Democracy Survive Globalization?" 20.

14. Luc de Barochez, "Europe: Le candidat va plus loin que le chef de l'Etat," *Le Figaro* (Paris), 7 March 2002.

15. Jean-Marie Guéhenno, "The Post-Cold War World: Globalization and the International System," *Journal of Democracy* 10 (January 1999): 24.

16. Friedman, *The Lexus and the Olive Tree*, 298.

17. Guéhenno, "The Post-Cold War World," 25.

CHAPTER SEVEN

1. Jacques Rupnik, "Eastern Europe: The International Context," *Journal of Democracy* 11 (April 2000): 122.

2. Joschka Fischer, "From Confederacy to Federation: Thoughts on the Finality of European Integration," speech at Humboldt University, Berlin, 12 May 2000.

3. Jacques Chirac, "Our Europe," speech to the Bundestag, Berlin, 27 June 2000.

4. Tony Blair, speech to the Polish Stock Exchange, Warsaw, 6 October 2000.

5. *Federalist* No. 20 asserts that "a sovereignty over sovereigns, a government over governments, a legislation for communities, as contradistinguished from individuals, as it is a solecism in theory, so in practice it is subversive of the order and ends of civil polity." Alexander Hamilton, James Madison, John Jay, *The Federalist Papers*, ed. Clinton Rossiter (New York: New American Library, 1961), no. 20, p. 138.

6. Desmond Dinan, ed., *Encyclopedia of the European Union*, updated edition (Boulder, CO.: Lynne Rienner, 2000).

7. Philippe C. Schmitter, *How to Democratize the European Union . . . and Why Bother?* (Lanham, MD: Rowman & Littlefield, 2000), 15–19.

CHAPTER EIGHT

1. John Ruggie, "Territoriality and Beyond: Problematizing Modernity in International Relations," *International Organization* 47 (Winter 1993): 139–74.

2. See Charles Tilly, "Reflections on the History of European State-Making," in Charles Tilly, ed., *The Formation of National States in Western Europe* (Princeton: Princeton University Press, 1975).

3. See, for example, Peter Koslowski, "Fatherland Europe? On European and National Identity and Democratic Sovereignty," in Andreas Follesdal and Peter Koslowski, eds., *Democracy and the European Union* (Berlin, Germany: Springer Verlag, 1998).

4. For a fuller discussion of the emergence of the modern concept of sovereignty, see Jeremy A. Rabkin, *Law without Nations? Why Constitutional Government Requires Sovereign States* (Princeton: Princeton University Press, 2005), especially pp. 45–70.

5. Juan J. Linz and Alfred Stepan, *Problems of Democratic Transition and Consolidation: Southern Europe, South America, and Post-Communist Europe* (Baltimore: Johns Hopkins University Press, 1996), 28.

6. One of the clearest statements of this point of view may be found in Philippe C. Schmitter, *How to Democratize the European Union . . . and Why Bother?* (Landham, MD: Rowman & Littlefield, 2000). See especially chapter 1.

7. Alexander Hamilton, James Madison, and John Jay, *The Federalist Papers*, ed. by Clinton Rossiter (New York: New American Library, 1961).

8. J. H. H. Weiler, Epilogue, "Fischer: The Dark Side," in Christian Joerges, Yves Mény, and J. H. H. Weiler, eds., *What Kind of Constitution for What Kind of Polity? Responses to Joschka Fischer* (San Domenico di Fiesole, Italy: Robert Schuman Centre for Advanced Studies, 2000).

9. Robert Cooper, *The Postmodern State and the World Order* (London: DEMOS and the Foreign Policy Centre, 1996).

10. Even Philippe Schmitter, one of the most thoughtful "non-state" theorists, acknowledges that if the EU were to play a more active role in security and defense policy, it would "have to acquire far more 'statelike' properties than it currently has in order to coordinate and finance such a collective effort." Schmitter, *How to Democratize the European Union*, 27.

11. Pierre Manent, "Democracy Without Nations?" *Journal of Democracy* 8 (April 1997): 92–102. See also Pierre Manent, "Les problèmes actuels de la démocratie," *Commentaire* 98 (Summer 2002): 261–68; and Pierre Manent, *Cours familier de philosophie politique* (Paris: Fayard, 2001), especially chapters 4–7 and 18. The latter work has now been published in English under the title *A World beyond Politics? A Defense of the Nation-State* (Princeton: Princeton University Press, 2006).

CHAPTER NINE

1. John G. Ruggie, J. Douglas Gibson Lecture, Queen's University, ON, Canada, 20 November 2000, available at: www.queensu.ca/sps/conferences_events/lectures/j_douglas_gibson/gibson_2000_ruggie.pdf.

2. Obviously, individual Americans hold a wide variety of views about the issues discussed in this chapter, and most American experts on international organizations probably disagree with much of what I have to say. In generalizing about what "Americans believe," I am referring to an outlook deeply rooted in the history and the constitutional order of the United States and perhaps best reflected in the predominant views in the U.S. Congress on these matters.

3. Abraham Lincoln, Letter to Henry L. Pierce & Others, Springfield, IL, 6 April 1859, http://showcase.netins.net/web/creative/lincoln/speeches/pierce.htm.

4. Robert Kagan, "Power and Weakness," *Policy Review* 113 (June/July 2002): 3–28.

5. Amitai Etzioni, *From Empire to Community* (New York: Palgrave Macmillan, 2004), 116–17.

6. John Locke, *Second Treatise of Government*, ed. by C. B. Macpherson (Indianapolis: Hackett Publishing Company, Inc., 1980), ch. 6, sec. 54, p. 31. Hereafter, all references to the *Second Treatise* include both the chapter and section numbers that are common to all editions, along with the page number of the Macpherson edition. I have not followed the frequent use of italics in the Macpherson edition. All italics used in citations from Locke reflect my own emphasis, as is noted parenthetically in the text.

7. Locke, *Second Treatise*, Ch. 2, sec. 6, p. 9.

8. Locke, *Second Treatise*, Ch. 9, sec. 123, pp. 65–66; ch. 9, sec. 124, p. 66; ch. 9, sec. 126, p. 66; ch. 9, sec. 127, p. 66; ch. 9, sec. 131, p. 68; ch. 11, sec. 136, p. 71.

9. Locke, *Second Treatise*, Ch. 9, sec. 128, p. 67.

10. Locke, *Second Treatise*, Ch. 9, sec. 129, p. 67; ch. 11, sec. 139, p. 74.

11. Locke, *Second Treatise*, Ch. 11, sec. 134, pp. 69–70

12. Locke, *Second Treatise*, Ch. 16, sec. 177, p. 92; ch. 16, sec. 178, p. 93; ch. 16, sec. 192, p. 98.

13. Thomas Hobbes, *Leviathan*, ed. by C. B. Macpherson (London: Penguin Books, 1985), ch. 20, p. 252. Hereafter, all references to the *Leviathan* include the chapter numbers that are common to all editions, along with the page number of the Macpherson edition.

14. Locke, *Second Treatise*, Ch. 16, sec. 196, p. 100.

15. Locke, *Second Treatise*, Ch. 16, sec. 192, p. 98.

16. Locke, *Second Treatise*, Ch. 19, sec. 226, p. 114; ch. 19, sec. 239, p. 122

17. Hobbes, *Leviathan*, ch. 18, p. 230.

18. Locke, *Second Treatise*, Ch. 8, sec. 95, p. 52; ch. 8, sec. 116, p. 62.

19. Locke, *Second Treatise*, Ch. 2, sec. 14, p. 13; ch. 5, sec. 45, p. 28.

20. Hobbes, *Leviathan*, ch. 13, p. 188.

21. Locke, *Second Treatise*, Ch. 1, sec. 3, p. 8;

22. Hobbes, *Leviathan*, ch. 21, pp. 268–70.

23. Locke, *Second Treatise*, Ch. 13, sec. 155, p. 81.

CHAPTER TEN

1. Arch Puddington, "The 2006 Freedom House Survey: The Pushback Against Democracy," *Journal of Democracy* 18 (April 2007): 125–38.

2. In the words of Iran's supreme leader Ali Khamenei, "Day by day, the reputation of liberal democracy and of America—the vanguard of liberal democracy in the world—is diminished in the eyes of the world." Translated by MEMRI. (Special Dispatch—Iran, 28 March 2007, no. 1523).

3. George W. Bush, Second Inaugural Address, 20 January 2005, available at www.whitehouse.gov/inaugural/.

4. The National Security Strategy of the United States of America, March 2006, available at www.whitehouse.gov/nsc/nss/2006/.

5. For a persuasive argument that not only democracy itself but democracy promotion has now become an "international norm," see Michael McFaul, "Democracy Promotion as a Universal Value," *The Washington Quarterly* 28 (Winter 2004–2005): 147–63.

6. Ivan Krastev, "The Anti-American Century?" *Journal of Democracy* 15 (April 2004): 5–17.

7. For example, see an article by the EU High Representative for the common foreign and security policy: Javier Solana, "Europe's Leading Role in the Spread of Democracy," *Financial Times*, 14 March 2005.

Index

Credits

Chapter 1 and chapter 10 are appearing for the first time. The remaining chapters have been published previously, as follows: chapter 2 as "The Democratic Moment," *Journal of Democracy* 2 (October 1991): 34–46; chapter 3 as "Human Rights," in Seymour Martin Lipset, ed., *The Encyclopedia of Democracy*, Vol. 2 (Washington, D.C.: Congressional Quarterly, 1995), 573–78; chapter 4 as "Liberalism and Democracy: Can't Have One Without the Other," *Foreign Affairs* 77 (March–April 1998): 171–80; chapter 5 as "From Liberalism to Liberal Democracy," *Journal of Democracy* 10 (July 1999): 121–34; chapter 6 as "Globalization and Self-Government," *Journal of Democracy* 13 (July 2002): 54–67; chapter 7 as "Understanding the European Union: Competing Goals, Conflicting Perspectives," *Journal of Democracy* 14 (October 2003): 42–56; chapter 8 as "Sovereignty and Democracy," *Policy Review*, no. 122 (December 2003–January 2004): 3–18; and a condensed version of chapter 9 as "Two Kinds of Internationalism," *The National Interest* 79 (Spring 2005): 84–92, and a full version as "Internationalism and Democracy," *Philosophy* 80 (October 2005): 495–512.

This previously published material is presented largely as it initially appeared, with only such minor changes as adding an occasional note and deleting a few short passages to avoid duplication. I am grateful to the publishers of these works for granting permission to reprint.